CUCINA AMORE

Nick Stellino

DOUBLEDAY
NEW YORK • LONDON • TORONTO • SYDNEY • AUCKLAND

PUBLISHED BY DOUBLEDAY
a division of Bantam Doubleday Dell Publishing Group, Inc.
1540 Broadway, New York, NY 10036

DOUBLEDAY and the portrayal of an anchor with a dolphin
are trademarks of Doubleday, a division of
Bantam Doubleday Dell Publishing Group, Inc.

Book design by Connie Lunde

Library of Congress Cataloging-in-Publication Data
Stellino, Nick.
Cucina amore / Nick Stellino.
p.   cm.
Includes index.
1. Cookery, Italian.   2. Cucina Amore (Television program)
I. Title.
TX723.S795   1995
641.5945—dc20   94-35639
                                         CIP
ISBN-0-385-47832-1
Copyright © 1995 by West 175 Enterprises, Inc.
All Rights Reserved
Printed in the United States of America
June 1995

3   5   7   9   10   8   6   4   2

PROUD SPONSORS OF THE CUCINA AMORE TELEVISION SERIES

ACKNOWLEDGMENTS

While it's easy for me to look ahead in search of new adventures, I find it hard to look back and frankly assess the importance of others' help in the accomplishing of my goals. I'd like to fantasize that I was a lone man driven by burning ambition. But the truth is quite different: I was a lucky man in the right places at the right times, and I wouldn't have been in those places at those times if it weren't for the following people.

Grazie to my mother, Massimiliana Boccato, and my father, Vincenzo Stellino, for showing me the way. Thanks to my brother, Mario Stellino, for believing that it could actually happen.

Thanks to Kaduri Shemtov for taking a chance with me; to Franco and Nina Cardone for letting my cooking shine in their kitchen; to Giancarlo Macchiarella for his generosity and his guidance in my early years; to Celestino Drago for letting me be part of a fabulous team and giving me a great sense of accomplishment (Celestino, you've been a great teacher and a great friend and I'll never forget it!); and to my teammates Craig D'Alessandro, Alex Lombardo, Tanino Drago, Giacomino Drago and Calogero Drago for making me part of their team.

I'm grateful to the team at West 175 Enterprises for seeing a story worth publishing in my dreams, especially John McEwen for leading the team with courage and enthusiasm; to John McLean for channeling the concept into a feasible day-to-day operation through the essential help of all his team members: Pattye O'Connor, Pam Brown, Marlene Lambert, Melissa Dungan, Leesa Wright and Natalie Johnson; and to Warren Roberts for his expertise in international marketing. Special thanks to Judy Kern, for her knowledgeable comments as Senior Editor from Doubleday; Christina Rylko, a mother, a wife and a superb project coordinator; to Suzanne Thostenson for editing my stories with a loving hand; and to Connie Lunde for translating my dreams into visual reality with her book design.

Now, let me take just a moment to express my appreciation to the most important person of all: my best friend and wife, Nanci Stellino. Thank you for letting me fly when others would have pulled me back; for risking it all with me, without hesitation; and for being there and holding me when I thought I'd lost it all. When I look at you I'm never afraid of what's ahead. "La paura del mondo si spegne nella luce dei tuoi occhi." "The fear of the world is obscured by the light in your eyes."

Finally I'd like to thank you, the reader, for choosing this book and even more for trying one or two of my recipes. My best wishes to all of you for all your culinary adventures.

CONTENTS

❦

Io Mi Ricordo ("I Remember")

The aroma of food cooking on the stove runs through my life like a soundtrack of melodies through a movie. So many of my life recollections seem directly connected to some kind of culinary experience. I can see the faces and hear the laughter from meals shared with loved ones who are no longer among us.

I see the creases in my Uncle Giovanni's face as he lights up his toothless smile. He was always happiest with a bowl of his favorite Minestra de Fasoi soup, a loaf of freshly baked bread and a glass of his homemade Ombretta red wine. I remember him standing over Grandma Adele's stove, lamenting the soup's excessive pepper, a concession she made when my father, Vincenzo il Sicilian (Vincent the Sicilian), was sitting at her table. Giovanni would hold the sides of his head and look up at the sky in mock desperation, then he'd flash that smile.

I remember my brother, Mario, and I fighting over a bowl of mascarpone cheese and some of my Mother's leftover Tiramisú cake. My mother always let me stand next to her on a stool pulled close to the stove when she cooked my favorite Western meal, Ragú di Carne Miste.

> *"The aroma of food cooking on the stove runs through my life like a soundtrack of melodies through a movie."*

GRANDFATHER DON NICOLA STELLINO, MY MOTHER AND I.

GRANDMA MARIA

"When I came to America to start a great new adventure, I started to cook because food kept me in touch with these faces, places, events, joys and tragedies that I left behind."

I remember watching my Mother's sister, Aunt Buliti, dancing the twist with her girlfriends without a care in the world, while munching on slices of Pizza Marguerita from the bakery down the street. When Aunt Buliti took Mario and me to the public gardens, we always stopped for la Brioscia con Gelato, a freshly baked sweet brioche roll split in half, filled with ice cream and topped with fresh whipped cream.

I can picture my father sweating over a hot grill with the sun blazing down as he lovingly basted grilled lamb chops with il Pesto d'Enzino, a magic potion of a marinade made with tomatoes, mint and garlic.

Sitting under a shade tree and shelling fresh peas into a wooden bowl on her lap, Grandma Adele told me stories of people and places from her youth. Through her eyes I saw the lantern-lit dance halls swirling with polkas played by a band of musically passionate local farm hands. The picture of her enjoying a moonlight moment came alive, and suddenly she looked like a young girl to me.

At the country house of my paternal grandmother, Grandma Maria, the whole family would gather around the table giggling in anticipation of her culinary masterpieces, which she carried to the table with little droplets of sweat covering her round jovial face. I can feel her soft hand caressing the top of my head and the warmth from one of her hugs.

When I came to America to start a great new adventure, I started to cook because food kept me in touch with these faces, places, events, joys and tragedies that I left behind. I continued to cook because it helped those thoughts and teachings stay alive in my heart, my mind and in my food.

Cucina Amore, Kitchen and Love, is not just a name for this book. It's a theme that summarizes my heartfelt devotion toward food, its flavor and its preparation. I know that the making of good food can bring family and friends together around the table in a great form of communication. Nothing stands in the way of a person's passion and the food that comes from that love.

My ambition here is to give you, the reader, a series of fun, flavorful and easy-to-prepare recipes. All of the ingredients are easily available from your local supermarket or Italian delicatessen. The only ingredient missing is your passion. But this has to come from within you, and it's a magic that will make your meals come alive with new meaning.

I will be very happy if a recipe or two from this book becomes part of a special event in your life and the people around you. Through these moments I believe there will always live on a little bit of Grandma Maria's hugs, Grandma Adele's Minestra de Fasoi, Uncle Giovanni's Ombretta, Aunt Buliti dancing the twist, Mother Massimiliana's Tiramisú, Don Enzino's Pesto and my brother, Mario's, mischievous smile.

Enough said now! Get on with the cooking. Buon Appetito!

THE TRADITIONAL HEALTHY MEDITERRANEAN DIET PYRAMID

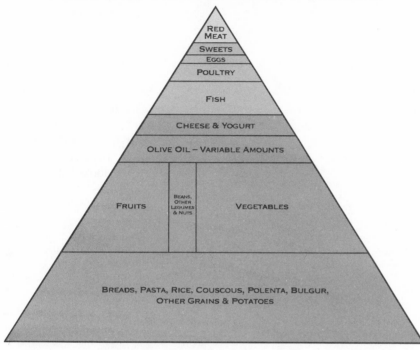

RED MEAT

SWEETS

EGGS

POULTRY

FISH

CHEESE & YOGURT

OLIVE OIL – VARIABLE AMOUNTS

FRUITS | BEANS, OTHER LEGUMES & NUTS | VEGETABLES

BREADS, PASTA, RICE, COUSCOUS, POLENTA, BULGUR, OTHER GRAINS & POTATOES

©1994 Oldways Preservation & Exchange Trust and The Mediterranean Diet Cookbook by Nancy Harmon Jenkins.

REGULAR PHYSICAL ACTIVITY.
WINE IN MODERATION (OPTIONAL).

A few times per week (or somewhat more often in very small amounts).
A few times per week.
Daily.

This pyramid illustrates the daily balance of food groups in the traditional Mediterranean diet of Crete, Greece and southern Italy circa 1960.

Groundbreaking research presented at the 1993 International Conference on the Mediterranean Diet at the Harvard School of Public Health supports the theory that this diet is one of the healthiest in the world. People who lived in the Mediterranean and ate this way had among the lowest incidence of heart disease, cancer, diabetes, and other chronic illnesses in the world.

Chef Stellino urges that his readers try to use his recipes within the pyramid's recommended daily balances.

For your own copy of a poster, send $5.00 to the Oldways Preservation and Exchange Trust, 45 Milk Street, Boston, MA, 02109.

ANTIPASTI

Appetizers

BRUSCHETTA AL POMODORO E BASILICO

TOASTED BREAD WITH TOMATOES AND BASIL

Serves 4

INGREDIENTS

6 Roma tomatoes, diced
2 garlic cloves, chopped
2 whole garlic cloves, peeled
3 tablespoons extra virgin olive oil
2¼ teaspoons balsamic vinegar
2 tablespoons chopped fresh basil
½ teaspoon salt
¼ teaspoon pepper
8 slices Italian bread, about ¾-inch thick
2 tablespoons grated Parmigiano Reggiano cheese (optional)

In a medium bowl, toss the tomatoes, chopped garlic, oil, vinegar, basil, salt and pepper until well mixed and let sit at room temperature for at least 20 minutes to let the flavors mingle. You can store the mixture in the refrigerator for up to 3 hours, but after that, the tomatoes will become too soft.

Toast the bread slices under a broiler until the edges are brown on both sides, but still white in the middle. Remove from the oven and when cool enough to handle, rub both sides of the bread with the whole garlic cloves until the cloves are too small to hold with your fingers.

Lay the bread slices on an ovenproof serving plate and top with the tomato mixture. Sprinkle a little of the cheese on top and place it quickly under the hot broiler until the cheese melts. Serve immediately.

What I remember best about visiting my paternal grandmother, Nonna Maria, every Sunday is bruschetta, cooked over hot coals on an iron grill in her wood burning oven. My recipe is a simpler adaptation of hers that

still possesses some of that special quality Nonna Maria always gave to her food.

Olive oil is an important flavoring agent in this recipe so I must ask you to use the best fruity, extra virgin olive oil you can find.

Massimilliana, my mother, was a Northerner who had to adapt to a whole new culture when she married my father and came to Sicily. Nonna Maria, my father's mother, was a spectacular cook who set an unusually high standard of excellence for my mother. Mamma fearlessly cultivated a style all her own and I think in many cases surpassed her cooking tutors.

This is Mamma's recipe for Caponata. It's a dish as Sicilian as Palermo, with her touch from the North. Serve it as an appetizer with toasted garlic bread slices, as a relish for grilled meats or as a condiment on sandwiches.

Serves 4

INGREDIENTS

1½ pounds eggplant, diced into ½-inch cubes
1¾ teaspoons salt
5 tablespoons olive oil
1½ cups diced onions
1 tablespoon chopped garlic
1 cup finely diced celery, parboiled for 2 minutes
¼ teaspoon red pepper flakes
¼ cup drained capers
4 ounces Sicilian or Greek pitted black olives, sliced in half
2 cups Tomato Sauce (see page 137)
3 tablespoons chopped fresh basil
¼ teaspoon unsweetened cocoa powder
2 tablespoons balsamic vinegar
1 tablespoon sugar

Preheat the oven to 450° F. Put the eggplant into a metal colander, sprinkle with 1 teaspoon of the salt, cover with a dish, put a heavy weight on top and let it drain for 15 minutes. Remove and pat very dry.

Pour 3 tablespoons of the olive oil into a large, ovenproof skillet and cook on high heat for 3 minutes. Reduce the heat to medium, add the eggplant and cook on one side for 4 minutes. Turn over and cook the other side for 4 minutes. Sprinkle with ½ teaspoon of the salt and bake in the preheated oven for 5 minutes. Remove from the oven and transfer the eggplant to a bowl to cool. Wipe the skillet, pour in the remaining 2 tablespoons of oil and cook on medium heat for 2 minutes. Add the onions, stir until well coated and cook for 4 minutes. Add the garlic, celery, red pepper flakes and ¼ teaspoon of the salt and cook for 3 minutes. Add the capers, olives, tomato sauce, basil and eggplant. Bring to a boil and cook for 3 minutes. Stir in the cocoa powder until well mixed and simmer for 3 minutes.

In a small pan on high heat, cook the vinegar and sugar until reduced by half and quite syrupy, about 2 minutes. Stir into the vegetables, mix well and simmer on very low heat for 4 minutes. Remove from the heat, transfer to a bowl and refrigerate overnight. Bring to room temperature before serving.

MELANZANE ARROSTE SOTTOACETO

ROASTED EGGPLANT IN BALSAMIC VINEGAR

Serves 4

INGREDIENTS

1 large eggplant, cut into ½-inch-thick slices
½ teaspoon salt
⅓ cup + 8 tablespoons olive oil
¼ teaspoon pepper
2 tablespoons chopped garlic
2 tablespoons chopped fresh basil
2 tablespoons chopped fresh mint
8 tablespoons balsamic vinegar

Preheat the oven to 425° F.

Sprinkle the eggplant slices with ¼ teaspoon of the salt and place them in a colander to drain for 20 minutes. Pat them with a paper towel until thoroughly dry.

Line the bottom of two large baking sheets with parchment paper. Brush the eggplant slices lightly on both sides with ⅓ cup of the olive oil and bake in the hot oven for 10 minutes. Turn them over and bake until they start to brown, about 10 minutes more. Remove from the oven and set aside.

In a small glass baking dish, place ⅓ of the eggplant slices, sprinkle with some of the salt, pepper, garlic, basil, mint, olive oil and vinegar, and repeat the process until all the eggplant is used. Cover with plastic wrap and let sit overnight in the refrigerator to ripen.

The next day, enjoy this dish for lunch or dinner, over salad greens, on toasted bread rubbed with garlic or sprinkled with a little goat cheese and bits of sun-dried tomatoes ... Mamma Mia!

This dish was present at all of the Stellino family picnics. Like many dishes, it tastes better the following day due to what I call "The Cinderella Effect": you combine plain, unsophisticated ingredients, and "bippity, boppity, boo," overnight, it blossoms into a beautiful culinary masterpiece.

In our household, this dish never lasted past the next day's lunch or dinner, so I've never been able to verify the exact length of its shelf life. I seriously doubt that you will be able to either!

Mamma's sister, Aunt Buliti, came to live with us when my brother, Mario, was born. She was very beautiful and also had a gift for cooking. This is my favorite recipe from my favorite aunt.

Serves 6

INGREDIENTS

2 (1-pound) eggplants, cut lengthwise into ¼-inch slices
¼ teaspoon salt
⅓ cup olive oil
8 ounces ricotta cheese
2 ounces fresh goat cheese
1 tablespoon grated Parmigiano Reggiano cheese
⅛ teaspoon garlic salt
⅛ teaspoon garlic powder
1 tablespoon chopped garlic

Place the eggplant slices in a colander and sprinkle with the salt. Put a plate on top, weight it down with a 28-ounce can of something and let it drain for 20 minutes.

Preheat the oven to 450° F.

Spread the eggplant out on a cutting board and pat very dry with a paper towel. Line a baking sheet with parchment paper, lay the eggplant slices on top, brush both sides lightly with the olive oil and bake for 20 minutes. Remove and let cool to room temperature.

While the eggplant is baking, in a large bowl stir together the ricotta cheese, goat cheese, Parmigiano Reggiano cheese, garlic salt, garlic powder and fresh garlic until the mixture has a uniform creamy texture.

Place a tablespoon of the cheese filling in the middle of each cooled eggplant slice and fold both edges over the top. Arrange on a plate and it's ready to serve.

CAVOLI ARRIMINATI

MIXED-UP CAULIFLOWER

Serves 4

INGREDIENTS

5 tablespoons raisins

4 tablespoons olive oil

1 pound fresh cauliflower florets, cut into 1-inch pieces,
parboiled and patted dry,

or 2 (10-ounce) packages frozen cauliflower florets, defrosted,
cut into 1-inch pieces and patted dry

4 garlic cloves, thinly sliced

¾ teaspoon salt

4 tablespoons pine nuts

¼ teaspoon red pepper flakes

1½ cups Tomato Sauce (see page 137)

½ cup water or Chicken Stock (see page 139)

$^{1}/_{16}$ teaspoon saffron powder

2 tablespoons balsamic vinegar mixed with 1 tablespoon sugar

½ teaspoon unsweetened cocoa powder

Place the raisins in a bowl of hot water to plump for 10 minutes. Drain and set aside.

Pour 2 tablespoons of the olive oil into a large nonstick skillet and heat on high until the oil is almost smoking, about 2-3 minutes. Add the cauliflower florets and cook for 2 minutes. Add the garlic, stir and cook for 2 minutes more. Sprinkle with ¼ teaspoon of the salt, transfer to a bowl and set aside.

Wipe the pan clean, raise the heat to medium-high, add the remaining oil, drained raisins, pine nuts and red pepper flakes and cook for 3-4 minutes. Add the cooked cauliflower, stir well and cook for 3 minutes. Add the remaining salt, the tomato sauce, water or stock, saffron, balsamic vinegar–sugar mixture and cocoa powder. Bring to a boil and simmer until most of the sauce has been absorbed, about 4-5 minutes.

Serve with slices of hearty Italian bread.

My grandmother, Nonna Maria, had a beautiful round face with big cheeks and a charming smile. She always let me stand on a chair to watch while she created world class meatballs and delicious vegetable dishes. My brother, Mario, and I, no great lovers of cauliflower, fell in love with this dish because it looks and tastes almost like a dessert.

My wife and I discovered this delightful dish on a long appetizer buffet in the middle of a small restaurant called La Veccia (The Old Lady) in the Veneto region of Italy. On one side of the room was an open kitchen run by three red-faced, gray-haired women and on the other, tables of happy chattering diners. Presiding over this colorful tableau was "La Vecchia," a bright-eyed, frail, white-haired woman who made sure everyone in the room knew one another before we even had our first glass of wine. For her customers, every meal was a family celebration.

Serves 4

INGREDIENTS

4 tablespoons olive oil
4 garlic cloves, sliced
2 onions, coarsely diced
2 tomatoes, peeled and coarsely diced
3 bell peppers, preferably green, red and yellow, seeded and coarsely diced
¼ teaspoon red pepper flakes
½ teaspoon salt
2 tablespoons chopped fresh parsley

Pour the oil into a large saucepan set on medium heat and cook the garlic until it starts to sizzle, about 2 minutes. Add the onions, reduce the heat to medium-low and cook for 3 minutes. Add the tomatoes, bell peppers, red pepper flakes and salt, cover and cook for 10 minutes, stirring once.

Uncover, reduce the heat to a simmer, and cook for 1 hour, stirring about every 10 minutes. Add the parsley and cook for 5 minutes. Remove from the heat and refrigerate the stew overnight. Bring it back to room temperature before serving to enjoy its complex flavors.

PEPERONI FARCITI

STUFFED PEPPERS

Serves 6

INGREDIENTS

3 bell peppers, preferably 1 yellow, 1 red, 1 green
1 recipe Stuffing (either Vegetarian on page 118 or Sausage on page 119)
1½ cups Chicken Stock (see page 139)
1½ cups Tomato Sauce (see page 137)
2 tablespoons grated Pecorino Romano cheese
2 tablespoons Italian Bread Crumbs (see page 142)

Preheat the oven to 375° F.

With a sharp knife, cut the peppers in half lengthwise and clean out the seeds. Stuff the peppers with your choice of stuffing. Place in a baking dish side-by-side. Pour the stock and tomato sauce into the baking dish. Sprinkle the top of the stuffed peppers with the cheese and bread crumbs. Bake until the peppers are soft, about 35-40 minutes. Serve warm. This dish tastes even better when you reheat it the next day.

COOK'S TIP

Sometimes I use the leftover sauce to top a pasta dish. If this idea appeals to you, increase the amounts of stock and tomato sauce each to 2 cups.

This recipe is the result of a long-standing family competition that started when my beloved Uncle Franz, a Hungarian expatriate, introduced us to stuffed peppers. Don Vincenzo, my father, not to be outdone by his brother-in-law, made his own Italian stuffed peppers. Then my mother entered the race and this recipe is my interpretation of her version. I only wish I could prepare it for Uncle Franz.

I became acquainted with this dish during my restaurant career. It makes a beautiful presentation and my version is quite simple to prepare. Once you familiarize yourself with the assembly technique, you'll be able to create your own variations on this very simple theme. Serve it as an appetizer or as an accompaniment to meat, chicken, or fish.

You can also use dried porcini mushrooms for this recipe. Let 2 tablespoons of dried porcini that have been broken into small pieces, soften in 1 cup of hot water and you're ready to go.

Serves 4

INGREDIENTS

2 tablespoons olive oil
2 ounces fresh or fresh-frozen porcini mushrooms, thinly sliced
2 ounces white mushrooms, thinly sliced
2 ounces fresh shiitake mushrooms, thinly sliced
⅛ teaspoon salt
1/16 teaspoon black pepper
2¼ teaspoons chopped shallots
1 garlic clove, chopped
¾ tablespoon chopped fresh parsley
1/16 teaspoon red pepper flakes
2 tablespoons sweet Marsala wine
2 large russet potatoes, peeled, shredded, patted dry
and mixed with ⅛ teaspoon of salt and pepper
2 tablespoons grated or shredded Parmigiano Reggiano cheese
or Swiss cheese, or both

Pour 1 tablespoon of the oil into an 8-inch nonstick sauté pan and heat on high until almost smoking, about 2 minutes. Add all the sliced mushrooms and cook 2 minutes, tossing once. Add the salt, pepper, shallots, garlic, parsley and red pepper flakes. Cook 1 more minute, tossing once. Add the Marsala wine and cook 2 more minutes or until the wine has completely evaporated. Place the mushroom mixture in a bowl and set aside.

Wipe the pan clean and add the remaining 1 tablespoon of oil. Heat on high until almost smoking, about 2 minutes. Put half the seasoned potatoes into the pan, pressing them down with the back of a spoon until they cover the whole bottom of the pan like a pancake. Make sure the potatoes are patted quite dry or the oil will splatter.

Reduce the heat to medium, top the potato pancake with the mushroom mixture and cheese. Add the remaining half of the shredded potatoes to form a second pancake on top of the mushroom filling. Press well on the edges to seal. Continue cooking on medium-low heat for 10 minutes. Turn the pancake over and cook the other side for 15 minutes, until well browned. If not brown enough, cook an additional 5 minutes on each side.

Cut into wedges and serve like a pie. If you wish to turn this into a Lucullian feast, add a dollop of sour cream to each serving and top with a little slice of truffle.

COOK'S TIP

I've never seen a better pancake "flipper" than Craig D'Alessandro at the Drago Restaurant in Santa Monica. He is so adroit that no one else is allowed to perform this trick. Chefs come from other restaurants to admire his magic.

It might be easier for you to turn the pancake onto a flat pan cover or dinner plate and then slide it back in the pan. But I encourage you to practice flipping because, once you get the hang of it, it will bring you great joy and satisfaction, not to speak of the admiration of your family and friends.

This is a fine little dish that also goes very well as a light entree at any meal. It is particularly good when served on top of toasted garlic bread, with a side dish of green peas and pancetta.

Serves 4

INGREDIENTS

4 tablespoons olive oil

4 onions, thinly sliced

4 garlic cloves, thinly sliced

½ teaspoon salt

⅛ teaspoon black pepper

⅛ teaspoon red pepper flakes

⅛ teaspoon oregano

1 (28-ounce) can peeled Italian tomatoes

1 tablespoon chopped fresh parsley

1 tablespoon chopped fresh basil

¼ chicken bouillon cube, crumbled

1 teaspoon chopped, dried porcini mushrooms

8 eggs

¼ teaspoon baking soda

4 tablespoons grated Pecorino Romano cheese (optional)

To make the onion/tomato relish, pour the olive oil into a large nonstick skillet and heat on medium until it sizzles. Add the sliced onions and cook until soft, tossing occasionally, for 3 minutes. Add the garlic, ¼ teaspoon of the salt, pepper, red pepper flakes and oregano. Cover, reduce the heat to low and cook until the onions start to turn brown, about 10 minutes, stirring occasionally. Make sure they don't burn.

Strain the tomatoes and chop them roughly. Save the juices to use later.

Increase the heat to medium-high. Add the tomatoes, parsley, basil, crumbled bouillon cube and porcini mushrooms and cook for 3 minutes.

Add the reserved tomato juice, bring to a boil and simmer until reduced to a sauce consistency, about 15 minutes. The relish can be prepared ahead to this point, then reheated to a simmer.

Break the eggs into a bowl. Add the baking soda, the remaining ¼ teaspoon of the salt and the cheese and beat well with a whisk. Add the eggs to the simmering sauce and cook, stirring continuously, until they're scrambled soft, about 3 minutes. Serve immediately.

FOCACCIA ALL'AGLIO E ROSMARINO

FOCACCIA WITH GARLIC AND ROSEMARY

Serves 6

INGREDIENTS

1 teaspoon sugar
1¼ cups warm water, about 100° F
1¼ tablespoons active dry yeast
3 cups all-purpose flour
½ teaspoon salt
3 tablespoons olive oil

TOPPING:

3 tablespoons olive oil
½ teaspoon salt, preferably freshly ground sea salt
¼ teaspoon pepper
3 tablespoons fresh rosemary leaves, crushed
2 tablespoons chopped garlic

To make the dough: Mix the sugar, warm water and yeast and let it rest for 5 minutes. In a large bowl, mix the flour and salt. Add the bubbling yeast mixture and the olive oil. Mix well until the dough forms a ball. Place the dough on a floured board and knead well for 10-15 minutes until it forms a smooth, elastic ball. Place it in a greased bowl, cover and let it rise in a warm, draft-free area for 1 hour.

Punch the dough down. Pat it into the shape you like best and place on a greased baking sheet or a pie pan. Stretch it out with your hands to make it fit. Make sure it is at least ½ inch thick. Cover and put it in a warm, draft-free place to rise again for about 30-45 minutes.

Preheat the oven to 500° F.

Make a series of small dimples on the surface of the dough with your fingers. Brush it with 2 tablespoons of the olive oil, sprinkle with the salt, pepper and fresh rosemary.

Reduce the oven temperature to 450° F and bake the focaccia for 12 minutes. Take it out and sprinkle with the chopped garlic, drizzle with the remaining olive oil and place it back in the oven for 5 more minutes, or until well browned.

Let it cool about 5-10 minutes. Cut into serving pieces and enjoy with your favorite Italian food.

When I was finally allowed to walk to school by myself, my feet always seemed to choose a different route through the beautiful city of Palermo. All routes, however, led to the "Panificio della Signora Rosa" (The Signora Rosa's Bread Shop), where I stopped each day for a slice of focaccia. Signora Rosa was not a sweet old lady. She was a complicated woman, at once mysterious, disagreeable and kind. I was fascinated and intimidated by her but we ultimately became friends. This focaccia reminds me that I miss her.

ZUPPE E INSALATE

Soups & Salads

L I C U R D I A

P O T A T O   A N D   O N I O N   S O U P

Serves 4 to 6

INGREDIENTS

2 pounds onions, finely diced
2 pounds white potatoes, finely diced
5 cups Chicken Stock (see page 139)
½ cup dry Marsala wine
1 teaspoon salt
¼ teaspoon pepper
2 tablespoons chopped fresh parsley
4 slices Italian bread, toasted and rubbed with garlic
2 tablespoons grated Romano cheese (optional)

Place the onions, potatoes, chicken stock, wine, salt, pepper and parsley in a large stockpot, cover and bring to a boil. Reduce the heat to its lowest setting and simmer for 1 hour, stirring every 10 minutes. Place one bread slice in the bottom of each bowl, pour the soup on top and sprinkle with the Romano cheese, if you wish.

We always spent summers with my maternal grandmother, Nonna Adele, up North in the Veneto region. Mario and I dreaded the long car trips home to Sicily in September. One year, we took the coastal route through

Calabria along a beautiful, unspoiled coastline. Mario and I begged to swim in the calm, blue sea and unexpectedly, my father agreed.

We developed an enormous hunger from playing in the water all morning and at lunchtime we turned our attention to a tiny diner near where we were parked. I will never forget that magnificent lunch. It was the first time I tasted the Calabrian version of potato and onion soup.

Zio Giovanni, Mamma's older brother and my favorite uncle, was, perhaps due to some genetic mishap, the worst cook in the family. His culinary contribution usually entailed trips to the ice cream store.

One day, to our horror, he decided to cook lunch. Before I could reason with him, he went out to the garden and came back with tomatoes and fresh herbs. He got out some stale bread, some of Grandma's chicken soup and some special olive oil.

What followed was culinary redemption for Zio Giovanni. His tomato soup became legend in our family – and we still got to go for ice cream.

Serves 4

INGREDIENTS

4 tablespoons + 4 teaspoons olive oil
1 onion, finely chopped
5 garlic cloves, thinly sliced
¼ teaspoon oregano
1 pound stale bread, cut into cubes
2 pounds fresh tomatoes, peeled and diced
1 (28-ounce) can peeled Italian tomatoes
2 cups Chicken Stock (see page 139)
½ teaspoon salt
¼ teaspoon pepper
3 tablespoons chopped fresh basil
2 tablespoons grated Romano cheese (optional)

In a large stockpot on medium heat, cook the 4 tablespoons of olive oil, the onion, garlic and oregano until the oil starts to sizzle. Reduce the heat to low and cook for 8 minutes, stirring occasionally. Add the bread, mix well, then add the fresh tomatoes, peeled Italian tomatoes, chicken stock, salt and pepper. Bring to a boil, then reduce the heat and simmer gently for 1 hour, stirring every 10 minutes. After 30 minutes, stir in the chopped basil.

Pour the soup into serving bowls and top each serving with a teaspoon of the olive oil and a sprinkle of the Romano cheese, if you wish. Tell your guests to stir and mash down the bread with their spoons, to get the best texture for their soup.

COOK'S TIP

The most flavorful bread would be from an Italian-style loaf, cut in slices, placed on a baking sheet, and left in a cold oven overnight. Rub the slices with garlic, then cut them into cubes to use in this recipe.

MINESTRA AMMUGGHIATA

MIXED-UP SOUP

Serves 6

INGREDIENTS

1 teaspoon salt
1 pound eggplant, diced
5 tablespoons olive oil
1 onion, diced
5 garlic cloves, thinly sliced
1 ounce dried porcini mushrooms, broken into small pieces
¼ teaspoon oregano
¼ teaspoon red pepper flakes
1 pound tomatoes, peeled and diced
6 cups Chicken Stock (see page 139)
2 tablespoons chopped fresh basil

Maria Rosa was the housekeeper for my boyhood friend Marco's family. She was an excellent, though untrained, cook who was able to turn traditional country fare into major culinary accomplishments.

The last year I saw her, I spent quite a bit of time asking about her recipes. She was generous with information and to my surprise, quite humble about her talent. What follows is one of her special soups of which I am particularly fond.

Grazie, Maria Rosa.

Sprinkle ¼ teaspoon of the salt over the eggplant, place in a colander with a plate and a 1-pound weight on top and let drain for 15 minutes.

In a large stockpot, cook the olive oil, onion, garlic, dried porcini, oregano and red pepper flakes, stirring often on medium heat until the onions start to sizzle, about 3 minutes. Cover and reduce to a slow simmer for 5 minutes.

Pat the eggplant pieces dry with a towel. Raise the heat to medium-high, uncover the stockpot and add the eggplant, stirring well for about 3 minutes. Add all of the other ingredients and bring to a boil. Reduce the heat to a slow simmer and cook, stirring every 10 minutes, for 1 hour. I find that if I place the cover on the pot and crack it open a bit for the first 25 minutes, the soup tastes a little bit better.

Place 3 cups of the soup in a blender and puree it to a smooth paste. Stir it back into the soup and simmer for 30 more minutes.

Please take a moment to thank Maria Rosa and enjoy your bowl of soup.

COOK'S TIP

When you use the blender to process hot liquids, secure the top firmly in place. Hold it down with a towel and start by pulsing on and off. Open the top to release the steam, then resecure the lid and pulse your way to a cream. Be very careful of the steam which can force off the lid if not released.

In the Venetian dialect, "fasoi" is the word for "beans." This type of soup is commonly known all over Italy as Minestra di Fagioli.

My grandmother Adele often prepared this delicacy for us. Every

time I prepare it myself, I feel as if she is with me, telling me when to stir or how much salt and pepper to put in, as she always did when I was a boy, eager to learn.

This simple soup packs quite a punch. It has a great flavor and is very filling. Enjoy it with a glass of ombretta (red wine) – Nonna Adele and I always did.

Serves 4 to 6

INGREDIENTS
4 tablespoons olive oil
4 garlic cloves, thinly sliced
¼ teaspoon red pepper flakes
¼ teaspoon oregano
1 tablespoon chopped fresh rosemary
½ onion, finely chopped
1 small carrot, peeled and finely diced
1 celery rib, finely diced
1 (28-ounce) can peeled Italian tomatoes
1 bay leaf
1 pound dried beans, preferably pinto,
soaked in water overnight or for a minimum of 12 hours
6½ cups Chicken Stock (see page 139)

Pour the oil into a large stockpot. Add the garlic, red pepper flakes, oregano, rosemary, onion, carrot and celery and cook over medium heat until the mixture starts to sizzle. Lower the heat to simmer, cover and cook for 5 minutes.

Drain the tomatoes, reserving the juice separately. Break up the tomatoes with your hands. Add the tomatoes and bay leaf to the stockpot. Cook over medium heat for 5 minutes, stirring often, until the tomatoes are almost dry. Add the beans, stirring to mix well, and cook 2 minutes. Add the chicken stock and reserved tomato juice, bring to a boil, reduce the heat to a simmer and cover, with the lid slightly ajar. Simmer 1½ hours, stirring every 15 minutes. After 1½ hours, transfer 4 cups of the soup to a blender and process until smooth. Stir it back into the rest of the soup and simmer 30 minutes more.

COOK'S TIP
Bean types all differ slightly in terms of their cooking time. This means that you should taste them for tenderness after 1 hour of cooking, retesting every 15 minutes.

ZUPPA DI PATATE E PEPERONI

SWEET PEPPER AND POTATO SOUP

Serves 4 to 6

INGREDIENTS
5 tablespoons olive oil
4 garlic cloves, thinly sliced
1 onion, finely chopped
¼ teaspoon thyme
¼ teaspoon red pepper flakes
2 pounds green, yellow, and red bell peppers (about 2 of each), diced
6 cups Chicken Stock (see page 139)
2 pounds new white rose potatoes, peeled and cubed
2 tablespoons chopped fresh parsley

Pour the oil into a large stockpot. Add the garlic, onion, thyme and red pepper flakes and cook over medium heat until the onion starts to sizzle. Reduce the heat to a simmer, cover and cook for 5 more minutes.

Uncover the pot and raise the heat to high. Add the diced peppers, stir well and cook for 2 minutes. Add the chicken stock and the potatoes and bring to a boil. Reduce to a simmer, cover and continue cooking for 30 minutes, stirring every 10 minutes. Pour 2 cups of the soup mixture into a blender and process until smooth. Stir this back into the rest of the soup mixture along with the parsley and simmer 15 minutes more.

Zia Ciccina, one of my father's favorite cousins, took over as culinary head of the family when Nonna Maria passed away. As the unofficial chronicler of our family history, she was my connection to a legendary Sicilian past I would never have heard of except from her. As we cooked in her kitchen, she told me stories in a tight Sicilian dialect I could hardly understand, while her smiling, expressive face and eyes made sure I got the meaning. She was the first one to make this wonderful soup for me.

STRACCIATELLA
EGG DROP SOUP

This family favorite is easy to prepare and very tasty. Its secret lies in the quality of the chicken stock. Canned stock will yield a good finished product, but a strong, homemade chicken stock will make it spectacular.

Serves 5

INGREDIENTS
9 cups Chicken Stock (see page 139)
3 eggs
5 tablespoons grated Parmigiano Reggiano cheese
1 tablespoon chopped fresh parsley
⅛ teaspoon nutmeg

Heat 8 cups of the stock in a stockpot set on medium heat. Mix the eggs and cheese in a bowl. Add the parsley, nutmeg and the remaining 1 cup of cold stock and mix well. When the stock is boiling, add the egg and cheese mixture, stirring with a whisk. Cook for 3 minutes, whisking continuously, over medium heat.

COOK'S TIP
If you want to make the soup a bit thicker, add either 3 tablespoons of semolina flour or 3 tablespoons of bread crumbs to the egg and cheese mixture before you pour it into the boiling stock.

INSALATA DI FUNGHI

MUSHROOM SALAD

Serves 4

INGREDIENTS

2 tablespoons olive oil

10 large white button mushrooms, quartered

4 tablespoons corn kernels, fresh or frozen and thawed

4 tablespoons peas, fresh or frozen and thawed

4 tablespoons fava or lima beans, fresh or frozen and thawed

2 tablespoons chopped fresh parsley

1 teaspoon chopped garlic

2 tablespoons white wine

4 tablespoons balsamic vinegar

½ teaspoon salt

4 ounces mixed baby salad greens (mesclun)

2 tablespoons finely chopped tomatoes

I have never been a voracious salad eater, but this dish is something I came up with for a small dinner party I was catering. The preparation is simple and the results are pleasing, especially for those who don't have a great deal of time to cook. Have fun and enjoy it!

Pour the oil into a large sauté pan and heat on high until it ripples and almost starts to smoke. Add the mushrooms and cook until brown on one side, about 3 minutes. Flip the mushrooms onto the other side and cook for 2 minutes. Add the corn, peas, beans, parsley and garlic and cook for 3-5 minutes.

Stir in the wine and cook until the wine is reduced to a glaze, stirring to make sure the vegetables don't stick. Turn off the heat and transfer the cooked vegetables to a bowl.

Deglaze the sauté pan with the balsamic vinegar over high heat and reduce by half, approximately 3-5 minutes. Pour the reduced vinegar over the salad greens, sprinkle with ¼ teaspoon salt and mix well. Distribute the baby salad greens among individual plates. Reheat the vegetable mixture over high heat in the sauté pan for 1 minute, then spoon on top of the salad greens. Sprinkle with just a bit of chopped tomatoes and the remaining salt. Eat and enjoy.

COOK'S TIP

When you sauté the mushrooms over high heat you want to sear them in their juices. To be successful, make sure the oil is sizzling hot before you add the mushrooms. Little details like this will make a big difference in the finished product.

Zio Giovanni used to say, "Non tutti i mali vengono per nuocere." This translates literally to, "Not all bad luck turns out to be bad." This recipe is a great example of that idea. It is a simple and easy variation upon

a delicious but complex classic, Peperonata, which I developed by mistake while trying to feed myself one frantically busy night while cooking at a restaurant.

Serves 4

INGREDIENTS
4 tablespoons olive oil
1 yellow onion, peeled and quartered
2 red bell peppers, seeded and cut into 1-inch squares
2 yellow bell peppers, seeded and cut into 1-inch squares
4 garlic cloves, chopped
2 tablespoons chopped fresh basil
2 tablespoons balsamic vinegar
4–5 ounces of mixed baby salad greens (mesclun)
¼ teaspoon salt
⅛ teaspoon pepper
3 tablespoons crumbled feta cheese

Pour half the olive oil into a medium nonstick skillet on high heat and cook until it almost reaches the smoking point. While the oil is heating, cut the onion quarters in half crosswise creating triangles. Cut off the ends and separate the layers with your hands.

When the oil is ready, add the onions and bell peppers and cook on high heat for 2 minutes. Flip the pieces over and cook for 2 more minutes. Add the garlic and basil and cook, stirring, for 1 minute. Add 1 tablespoon of the vinegar, stir and cook for 30 seconds, remove from the heat and transfer to a bowl.

In a large salad bowl, mix the greens with the remaining olive oil, remaining vinegar, the salt, pepper and feta cheese. Toss until everything is well coated. Divide the salad among the serving plates and top with the warm pepper-onion mixture.

INSALATA DI FUNGHI ALLA GRIGLIA

GRILLED MUSHROOM SALAD

Serves 4

INGREDIENTS

6 tablespoons extra virgin olive oil
3 tablespoons balsamic vinegar
¼ teaspoon salt
¼ teaspoon pepper
1 teaspoon chopped garlic
1 teaspoon chopped fresh basil
¾ pound shiitake mushrooms
or any combination of wild mushrooms
4 ounces mixed baby salad greens (mesclun)

In a bowl, mix the oil, vinegar, salt, pepper, garlic and basil, whisking well.

Cut the stems off the mushrooms and toss with the dressing in the bowl. Marinate at room temperature for 30 minutes to 1 hour.

Drain, reserving the dressing and mushrooms separately. Cook the mushrooms on a hot grill or on a baking sheet under the broiler, about 3 minutes on each side.

Mix the salad greens with the reserved dressing and top with the grilled mushrooms.

COOK'S TIP

When you grill the mushrooms, take care not to burn them. If the barbecue or broiler is too hot, 3 minutes might be too much – use your judgement. You could also cook the mushrooms in a nonstick sauté pan over high heat for about 2 minutes on each side.

If you don't have access to a variety of wild mushrooms, the fresh, flavorful shiitake mushrooms will make an excellent substitute.

PASTE E RISOTTI

Pasta & Risotto

PASTA AGLIO OLIO E PEPERONCINO

GARLIC AND OIL PASTA

Serves 4 to 6

INGREDIENTS

3 quarts water (salt optional)
½ cup olive oil
10 average-size garlic cloves, sliced
¼ teaspoon salt
¼ teaspoon red pepper flakes
3 tablespoons chopped fresh parsley
1 pound pasta – spaghetti or spaghettini
3 tablespoons grated Romano cheese

In a large stockpot, bring the water to a boil with or without the optional salt.

Pour the oil into a large sauté pan set on medium heat and cook the garlic until it starts to sizzle, about 3 minutes. Be careful not to let it turn brown and burn. Remove from the heat and add the salt, red pepper flakes and half the parsley.

Add the pasta to the boiling water and cook according to package directions until it's tender. Drain well and return the pasta to the pot. Pour the sauce over the pasta, add the remaining parsley and cook over medium heat, stirring well to coat the pasta with the sauce, about 3 minutes. Turn off the heat, add the cheese and toss to distribute the ingredients.

My *mother seemed to be always ready with a large selection of quick, easy and tasty meals. Some she developed by herself and others were passed on by her mother or other family and friends. This is one of my favorite*

quick fix dishes. The olive oil infused with the flavors of garlic and red pepper becomes the sauce that will coat the pasta.

Its simplicity is deceptive, however. Each step is like a well thought out equation in a math problem. Any departure from proper procedure and the dish loses its delicacy in a puddle of oil. The last step is the most crucial one. Its purpose is to coat each strand of pasta with the infused olive oil to produce a finished dish that will shine like a ripe tomato in the summer sun.

All of the ingredients should be well distributed in the final dish. Think of the pasta as the beautiful countryside, graced with a succession of curving hills, speckled with beautiful trees, ponds and farmhouses.

There are many stories about how this dish got its name. One version is that such a dish was, in the old days, a very typical fare of the southern coastal bordellos. Legend has it that during hard financial times local fishermen would pay for the pleasure of a "lady's company" with their catch, especially anchovies. The entrepreneurial "Grand Dame" of some such establishment found a way to turn frugality into culinary history, the result being the birth of this dish.

Serves 4 to 6

INGREDIENTS

3 quarts water (salt optional)
4 tablespoons olive oil
½ cup pitted Kalamata olives, cut in half
4 garlic cloves, sliced
1 tablespoon drained capers
1 tablespoon anchovy paste
¼ teaspoon red pepper flakes
2 tablespoons chopped fresh parsley
1¼ cups Chicken Stock (see page 139)
1 cup Tomato Sauce (see page 137)
1 pound pasta – ziti, penne or spaghetti
grated Pecorino Romano cheese (optional)

In a large pot, bring the water to a boil with or without the optional salt.

Pour the olive oil into a large sauté pan set on medium heat and cook the olives, garlic, capers, anchovy paste and red pepper flakes for 3 minutes, stirring well to dissolve the anchovy paste. Add the parsley, chicken stock and tomato sauce and bring to a boil. Simmer uncovered for 15-20 minutes, until the sauce is thick enough to coat the back of a spoon.

Meanwhile, add the pasta to the boiling water and cook according to package directions until just tender. Drain well and add it back to the pot. Pour the sauce on top of the pasta and cook over medium heat, stirring well to coat the pasta with the sauce, about 3 minutes. Sprinkle with the Romano cheese, if you wish.

COOK'S TIP

It's very important that cooked pasta not sit around waiting to be sauced as it will quickly develop a gummy texture. Always wait until the sauce is ready before cooking your pasta and toss the cooked pasta immediately with the sauce.

PASTA CON CAPPERI E ACCIUGHE

PASTA WITH CAPERS AND ANCHOVIES

Serves 4 to 6

INGREDIENTS

3 quarts water (salt optional)

1 pound pasta – rigatoni, tortiglioni or penne

8 tablespoons olive oil

4 garlic cloves, sliced

1 tablespoon anchovy paste

2 teaspoons capers

¼ teaspoon red pepper flakes

1 tablespoon chopped fresh parsley

2 teaspoons toasted Italian Bread Crumbs (see page 142)

2 tablespoons grated Romano cheese

In a large stockpot, bring the water to a boil with or without the optional salt. Cook the pasta according to package directions until just tender.

While the pasta is cooking, pour the oil into a large sauté pan set on medium-high heat and cook the garlic and anchovy paste until the garlic starts to sizzle, about 3 minutes, being careful not to let it burn. Add the capers, red pepper flakes and half of the parsley. Stir well and let the sauce rest.

Drain the pasta and put it back in the pot. Pour the sauce over the pasta, tossing over medium heat until well coated, for 2 minutes. Sprinkle with the remaining parsley and turn off the heat. Add the bread crumbs and cheese and toss well.

"La Pasta é Pronta." The pasta is ready.

COOK'S TIP

The toasting of the bread crumbs is important because it enhances the flavor of the dish. Just spread the bread crumbs over a preheated nonstick sauté pan and cook on high heat until they just darken in color, about 3 minutes, shaking the pan to make sure they don't burn.

Some of my happiest and most vivid memories are of times when my busy father took Mario and me fishing with Franco, a commercial fisherman from the village of Sferracavello, a few miles from Palermo.

On one fishing trip with Franco, the weather turned nasty. The sky was dark, the sea choppy and flashes of lightning filled the horizon. Franco's home was in the oldest part of the village where the streets were too narrow to drive. The rain was pouring down by the time we walked up the hill to Franco's door. Father cut a stoic figure, impervious to the rain, stepping into puddles up to his ankles. Mario and I danced in the puddles, faces up, drinking the rain as it fell.

Franco and his wife welcomed us into their small, sparsely furnished house, which was spotlessly clean and smelled of freshly baked bread and other wonderful foods, where we were treated to a memorable meal. It was a magical time when casual acquaintances came together and shared the warmth and pleasure of one another's company. It was also the occasion when I ate this pasta dish for the first time.

The ingredient that gives this dish its angry name is the red pepper flakes. But unless you use the full ¼ teaspoon, the pasta loses its full certification as the official "arrabbiata." This is a serious matter, not to be taken lightly.

Therefore, if you should even think about reducing the amount of red pepper, be sure not to announce the dish to your guests as "arrabbiata." It could, however, qualify for secondary certification, which would translate as "vivace" or "modestly upset."

What's the matter with you guys ... I'm just kidding! Enjoy this dish however you want!

Serves 4 to 6

INGREDIENTS

3 quarts water (salt optional)
4 tablespoons olive oil
4 garlic cloves, sliced
¼ teaspoon red pepper flakes
1½ cups Tomato Sauce (see page 137)
1 cup Chicken Stock (see page 139) or water
¼ teaspoon salt
3 tablespoons chopped fresh parsley
1 pound pasta – penne or ziti

Pour the water into a large stockpot with or without the optional salt and bring it to a boil.

While the water is heating, pour the oil into a large sauté pan set on medium heat and cook the garlic and red pepper flakes until the garlic starts to sizzle, about 2-3 minutes. Be careful not to let it burn. Add the tomato sauce, chicken stock or water, salt and 2 tablespoons of the parsley, bring to a boil and simmer for 5 minutes.

When the water is boiling, add the pasta and cook according to package directions until just tender. Drain well and return to the pot. Add the sauce, turn the heat up to medium-high and toss until it's well coated. Sprinkle with the remaining parsley and cook, stirring, for 1 minute.

COOK'S TIP

Chicken stock will make the flavor a bit more intense and the finish more saucy. If you do not want to use chicken stock, you could add about ½ cup of the pasta-cooking water during the simmering process. The finish and flavor will be just as good.

PASTA AL FILETTO DI POMODORI

FILLET OF TOMATOES PASTA

Serves 4 to 6

INGREDIENTS
3 quarts water (salt optional)
1 (28-ounce) can peeled Italian tomatoes
4 tablespoons olive oil
5 garlic cloves, sliced
⅛ teaspoon red pepper flakes
¼ teaspoon salt
¼ teaspoon black pepper
⅛ teaspoon oregano
10 leaves fresh basil, chopped, *or* 1 teaspoon dried
1 pound spaghetti
3 tablespoons grated Romano cheese

In a large stockpot, bring the water to a boil with or without the optional salt.

Strain the tomatoes, reserving the juice separately. Break the tomatoes into small pieces.

Pour the oil into a large sauté pan set on medium-high heat and cook the garlic and red pepper flakes for 3 minutes. Add the tomato pieces, shaking the pan gently to reduce the oil splatter, and cook for 3 minutes. Add the salt, black pepper, oregano and basil and cook, stirring occasionally, for 2 minutes. Add the reserved tomato juice, bring to a boil and simmer for 5 minutes. Add salt to taste.

Cook the pasta according to package directions until just tender. Drain and return to the pot.

Add the sauce to the pasta, stirring continuously to ensure even coating and cook for 3-5 minutes on medium heat. Turn off the heat, add the cheese and toss until it's distributed evenly.

COOK'S TIP
I think Italian canned tomatoes are far superior to anything else on the market. They're usually picked and canned when they're ripe and at the peak of flavor. The result is much sweeter than that produced by their American counterparts. Look for them in an Italian delicatessen.

My brother, Mario, and I always referred to my father as Don Vincenzo, the King of Pasta (even though my mother was Queen over all). The basis for this regal nickname came at least in part from his ability to prepare this incredibly delicious pasta dish out of a can!

I'm particularly fond of this recipe since it was the first I was allowed to prepare for the family under the guiding supervision of Don Vincenzo. It's a good choice for a Saturday or Sunday afternoon lunch.

Fillet of tomatoes is simply a fancy name for tomatoes that have been peeled and seeded.

PASTA ALLA NORMA

PASTA WITH EGGPLANT AND TOMATO SAUCE

This style of pasta is often called "Sicilian style" or "alla Norma" which is an expression that means it was done "by the rules" or according to tradition.

Eggplant is an important part of southern Italy's culinary tradition where its versatility is properly honored. The following recipe is fabulously simple, yet enormously satisfying. The eggplant is quickly sautéed and then braised to perfection in the tomato sauce to obtain the perfect combination of flavors.

This dish is traditionally served with scamorza, smoked mozzarella, which is readily available at Italian delicatessens. Otherwise, substitute grated salted ricotta, another specialty cheese item.

Serves 4 to 6

INGREDIENTS

2 cups cubed eggplant
½ teaspoon salt
3 quarts water (salt optional)
2 tablespoons olive oil
1 teaspoon chopped garlic
¼ teaspoon red pepper flakes
⅛ teaspoon black pepper (optional)
2 cups Tomato Sauce (see page 137)
1 cup Chicken Stock (see page 139) or water
3 tablespoons chopped fresh basil
1 pound pasta – penne or ziti
5 ounces smoked mozzarella cheese (Scamorza), cubed

Place the eggplant in a colander, sprinkle it with ¼ teaspoon of the salt, mix well, cover with a weighted plate and let drain for about 15 minutes (the salt will drain the bitter water from the eggplant). Pat the eggplant cubes dry.

Pour the water into a large pot with or without the optional salt and bring it to a boil.

While the water is heating, pour the oil into a large nonstick sauté pan set on high heat and cook until it starts to ripple and is almost smoking. Add the eggplant, cook for 2 minutes, stir and cook for 1 minute. Add the garlic, red pepper flakes, remaining salt and pepper, if desired, and cook for 1 minute. Stir in the tomato sauce, chicken stock or water, and basil, bring to a boil, reduce the heat and simmer for 20 minutes.

Cook the pasta in the boiling water according to package directions until al dente or just tender. Drain, return it to the pot and add the sauce. Toss until well coated and cook over medium heat for 2 minutes. Turn off the heat, add the smoked mozzarella and toss well.

PASTA CON LE ZUCCHINE

ZUCCHINI PASTA

Serves 4 to 6

INGREDIENTS

3 quarts water (salt optional)
8 tablespoons olive oil
4 medium zucchini, sliced thin and patted dry
2 tablespoons chopped garlic
4 teaspoons chopped fresh mint
4 teaspoons chopped fresh basil
¼ teaspoon salt
¼ teaspoon red pepper flakes
¼ teaspoon black pepper (optional)
1 pound pasta – rigatoni, tortiglioni or penne
2 tablespoons grated Romano cheese

Bring the water to a boil in a large stockpot with or without the optional salt.

Pour the oil into a large sauté pan set on high and heat until it starts to ripple and almost smokes, about 3 minutes. Add the sliced zucchini, being careful to avoid oil splatters and cook until the edges start to turn brown, stirring occasionally to prevent sticking, about 3 minutes. Turn the zucchini over and cook for 3 more minutes. Sprinkle with the garlic, mint, basil, salt, red pepper and optional black pepper (for those of us who like an "extra kick") and cook for 2 minutes, stirring often to make sure the garlic doesn't stick and burn. Remove from the heat and set aside.

Cook the pasta according to package directions until just tender.

While the pasta is cooking, remove 1 cup of the pasta cooking water and add it to the zucchini mixture in the sauté pan. Return to high heat and deglaze the pan, scraping to loosen the brown bits that stick to the bottom. Cook until the water turns a light brown color, about 2 minutes.

Drain the pasta and return it to the pot. Add the sauce to the pasta and cook over medium heat, stirring until well coated, about 2 minutes. Be careful that nothing sticks to the bottom of the pan. Sprinkle with the cheese and toss well to distribute evenly. The dish is now ready to be served.

Like most little boys, my brother, Mario, and I showed minimal interest in the culinary appreciation of vegetables. My mother, being a lady of great resourcefulness, always tried to find a way of incorporating a healthy dose of vegetables into our daily diet. I'm not saying she was always successful, for we could smell anything resembling a vegetable a mile away, but most of the time she succeeded at fooling our young palates into actually liking vegetables, especially when they were presented in a recipe like this one.

I suggest you use rigatoni, tortiglioni or penne pasta because these shapes have ridges along their surfaces that maximize their ability to grab onto the sauce.

In 1984, I rediscovered the beautiful Veneto region of my childhood with my wife, Nanci. One day on our way to Ferrara we stopped for a quick plate of pasta at a nondescript truck stop. It was smoke-filled and noisy but Nanci found it charming and "so Italian" that we stayed. A round lady with a cherubic face dropped a carafe of a light, spunky Lambrusco at our table and left. By the time we got to our third carafe, our lunch had not arrived but we were having the time of our lives. Finally, our angel delivered the pasta she had chosen for us. I was amazed to find this delicious dish was made with radicchio, a bitter red lettuce I had always found unappetizing.

I've made the dish many times since, so I know that my delight with it was not due to the spells cast by wine and my beautiful wife.

Serves 4 to 6

INGREDIENTS

3 quarts water (salt optional)
2 tablespoons butter
3 tablespoons chopped garlic
2 tablespoons chopped shallots
½ cup chopped radicchio
¼ teaspoon salt
⅛ teaspoon pepper
¼ cup white wine
½ cup heavy cream
½ cup Chicken Stock (see page 139)
4 ounces Gorgonzola or Roquefort cheese, diced
1 pound pasta – rigatoni, tortiglioni or penne

Pour the water into a large stockpot with or without the optional salt and bring to a boil.

While the water is heating, cook the butter, garlic and shallots in a large sauté pan over medium heat until the garlic starts to sizzle, about 3 minutes. Add the radicchio and cook for 2 minutes. Add the salt and pepper and cook for 1 minute. Pour in the wine, deglaze the pan and reduce by a third, about 3 minutes.

Stir in the cream, chicken stock and cheese and bring to a boil, stirring well to make sure the cheese melts evenly and doesn't stick to the bottom. Reduce the heat, simmer for 4 minutes then turn off the heat.

Add the pasta to the boiling water and cook according to package directions until just tender. Reheat the sauce on medium heat. Drain the pasta, return it to the pot, add the sauce and cook for 2 minutes over medium heat, tossing continuously to make sure it's well coated and doesn't stick.

COOK'S TIP

Sharp tasting, imported Gorgonzola or Roquefort cheese is your best choice for this sauce. If, like me, you really enjoy the tangy taste, then at the end of the recipe, while the pasta is still hot, add another ⅓ cup of diced Gorgonzola and toss well.

PASTA AI FUNGHI DI BOSCO

WILD MUSHROOM PASTA

Serves 4 to 6

INGREDIENTS

3 quarts water (salt optional)

4 tablespoons olive oil

3 ounces fresh or fresh-frozen porcini mushrooms, diced, *or* ½ ounce dried, softened in ½ cup hot water for 30 minutes, drained and chopped

5 large white button mushrooms, about ½ pound, diced

4 ounces shiitake mushrooms, diced

4 garlic cloves, chopped

1½ tablespoons chopped fresh parsley

¼ teaspoon salt

⅛ teaspoon black pepper

⅛ teaspoon red pepper flakes

½ cup white wine

½ cup heavy cream

½ cup Tomato Sauce (see page 137)

1¼ cups Chicken Stock (see page 139)

1 pound pasta – penne, ziti, rigatoni or tortiglioni

Bring the water to a boil in a large stockpot with or without the optional salt.

Pour the olive oil into a large nonstick skillet and cook over high heat until it starts to sizzle, 3 minutes. Add all the diced mushrooms and cook for 1 minute. Stir well and cook 1 minute more. Add the garlic, 1 tablespoon of the parsley, the salt, black pepper and red pepper flakes, stir well and cook for 2 minutes, until the garlic is fragrant and the mushrooms are getting brown. Pour in the wine and cook 1 minute. Add the cream, tomato sauce, and chicken stock and bring to a boil. Reduce immediately to a simmer and cook for 10 minutes.

When the water is boiling, add the pasta and cook until al dente or just tender. Drain well, return to the pot and add the simmering sauce along with the remaining ½ tablespoon of parsley. Toss to coat well with the sauce. Cook over medium heat for 3 minutes and serve.

Fresh wild mushrooms were not an everyday staple in our diet, but if you were quick enough to snatch them there would always be a few available at the open markets, especially after the big rains.

Father was a master in the art of mushroom cooking. He'd grill, sauté or bake them; nothing limited his imagination. This particular pasta dish was quite a treat and always a welcome addition to our special-occasion dinners. It is one of a series of mushroom-based dishes that I'm confident will seduce even the most skeptical among you.

PASTA WITH PORCINI MUSHROOMS AND TOMATO

My family always went mushroom hunting right after the first fall rain. Our favorite haunt was an oak forest that used to belong to the King of Sicily, about 2 hours drive from Palermo. Our goal was "Il Porcino," the "King of all Mushrooms." Unfortunately, the professional mushroom hunters would often beat us to the royal prize, but if we found enough mushrooms to make this dish, we were happy. Today, you can hunt porcini more easily in the supermarket, where they may be called "cepe" or "boletus." Although porcini have a short season, the freshly frozen product is a good substitute.

Serves 4 to 6

INGREDIENTS

3 quarts water (salt optional)
4 tablespoons olive oil
5 garlic cloves, sliced
8 ounces fresh or fresh-frozen porcini mushrooms,
scrubbed and diced into ½-inch pieces, *or* 1½ ounces dried,
softened in ½ cup hot water for 30 minutes, drained and chopped
¼ teaspoon red pepper flakes
1 teaspoon salt
5 tablespoons white wine
5 large tomatoes, peeled and diced
4 tablespoons chopped fresh basil
1 pound pasta – fettuccine all'uovo, fettuccine verdi, spaghetti or tortiglioni
4 tablespoons grated Parmigiano Reggiano cheese

In a large pot, bring the water to a boil with or without the optional salt.

Cook the olive oil, garlic, porcini mushrooms and red pepper flakes in a large sauté pan set on medium heat for 3 minutes. Sprinkle with half of the salt and cook until the mushrooms are just starting to brown, about 2 minutes. Add the wine, deglaze the pan and cook on high heat until the wine reduces by half, about 3-5 minutes.

Stir in the tomatoes, basil and the remaining salt, bring to a boil and cook for 2 minutes. Reduce the heat and simmer for 3 minutes.

Cook the pasta in the boiling water until just tender. Drain well and return to the pot. Add the sauce to the pasta, toss until well coated and cook over medium heat for 2 minutes, until most of the juices have been absorbed. Turn off the heat, add the cheese, and toss until well coated. Enjoy.

COOK'S TIP

If you are using dried porcini mushrooms, soften them in ½ cup hot chicken stock instead of water and reserve the liquid to add to the sauce when you add the tomatoes. It will greatly enhance the flavor.

PASTA CON I PORCINI E LE VONGOLE

PASTA WITH CLAMS AND MUSHROOMS

Serves 4 to 6

INGREDIENTS

3 quarts water (salt optional)

4 tablespoons olive oil

4 garlic cloves, sliced

6 ounces fresh or fresh-frozen porcini mushrooms, cut into ½-inch dice,
or ½ ounce dried, softened in ½ cup hot water for 30 minutes,
drained and chopped

¼ teaspoon red pepper flakes

1½ pounds fresh clams, preferably Manila, well scrubbed, in their shells

1 teaspoon salt

1 cup white wine

1½ cups clam juice

½ cup Tomato Sauce (see page 137)

3 tablespoons chopped fresh Italian parsley

1 pound pasta – linguine or spaghetti

Pour the water into a large pot with or without the optional salt and
bring to a boil.

While the water is heating, pour the oil into a large sauté pan set on
medium-high heat and cook the garlic, mushrooms and red pepper flakes until
the garlic starts to sizzle, about 2-3 minutes. Add the clams and salt, stir until
well coated and cook for 2 minutes. Pour in the wine, raise the heat to high
and cook, covered, for 3 minutes. Remove the clams and set them aside in a
bowl. Discard any clams that did not open during cooking. Add the clam juice,
tomato sauce and parsley, bring to a boil and simmer, covered, for 10 minutes.

While the sauce is simmering, remove half the clams from their shells,
chop fine and set aside along with the clams still in their shells. Return the
clams to the sauce about 3 minutes before the pasta is finished cooking.

Cook the pasta in the boiling water according to package directions
until just tender. Drain and return to the pot. Add the sauce, turn the heat
to medium-high and cook the pasta until it has absorbed most of the juices,
stirring continuously until well coated, about 2 minutes. Remove the pasta
from the heat, pour into a large bowl and let it rest for 1-2 minutes. Bring it
to the table and serve it family style with lots of bread on the side.

Mastro Calogero de Francisci, a
widower in his sixties, lived in our
apartment building in Palermo. He
wore beautifully cut black suits with
perfectly rounded shoulders, lapels
rolling out to the last button hole and
pants squarely creased. He carried a
golden pince-nez in his breast pocket
behind an immaculate linen handker-
chief and he always called me
"Signorino" or "little lord."

One day he invited my father
and me to an impromptu lunch. The
way Mastro Calogero moved through
his magnificent kitchen reminded me
of Toscanini conducting a symphony
orchestra. What followed was this
dish: a banquet fit more for a king
than a signorino.

Nonna Adele, *my maternal grand-mother, was a very special lady. Even though she lived a very difficult life spanning two wars, she always radiated a gentle sweetness and shared a great sense of humor.*

Every summer my family traveled from Palermo in Sicily up to Nonna Adele's house in Contarina, a small town in the Veneto region. Sicily and Veneto were not only separated by a large territorial distance, but were culturally and historically worlds apart. Their local dialects were like two different languages. The weather was completely different, the land was different and people's philosophies of life were different.

One of the things that brought the disparate parts of our family together was our love and appreciation of food. I offer you now, Nonna Adele's favorite pasta dish that helped bridge the gap between two cultures.

Serves 4 to 6

INGREDIENTS

3 quarts water (salt optional)
4 tablespoons olive oil
4 garlic cloves, sliced
2 pounds live clams, Manila or littleneck, well scrubbed, in their shells
¼ teaspoon red pepper flakes
¼ teaspoon salt
1 cup white wine
1 cup clam juice
3 tablespoons chopped fresh parsley
½ cup Tomato Sauce (see page 137)
1 pound pasta – linguine, spaghetti or spaghettini

In a large pot, bring the water to a boil with or without the optional salt.

Pour the oil into a large sauté pan set on medium heat, and cook the garlic until it starts to sizzle, about 2 minutes. Add the clams, red pepper flakes and salt and cook for 1 minute. Add the wine and cook for 1 minute. Add the clam juice, parsley and tomato sauce and bring to a boil. Reduce to a simmer, cover the pan and cook until all the clams have opened, about 3-5 minutes.

Take the clams out of the sauce, place in a bowl and let them sit for a few minutes. Discard those that still haven't opened. Take half of the clams out of their shells and mince them. Add all the clams to the simmering sauce about 3 minutes before the pasta is done. Mix well and cover.

Add the pasta to the boiling water and cook according to package directions until just tender. Drain well and return to the pot. Add the sauce, toss to coat well and cook over medium heat 2-3 minutes. Most of the sauce should be absorbed.

COOK'S TIP

When you bring the clams home, put them in a bowl of cold water for 10-15 minutes and then drain them. Do this twice. It will help to clean out any grit, sand, and dirty water. Scrub the shells with a vegetable brush or plastic scrubber.

PASTA AL SALMONE AFFUMICATO

SMOKED SALMON PASTA

Serves 4 to 6

INGREDIENTS

3 quarts water (salt optional)

2 tablespoons butter

2 tablespoons chopped shallots

1 tablespoon chopped garlic

3 ounces smoked salmon, chopped

3 tablespoons vodka

¼ teaspoon salt

¾ cup heavy cream

¾ cup clam juice

3 tablespoons Tomato Sauce (see page 137)

5 tablespoons frozen peas, thawed

1 pound pasta – penne rigate or farfalle (bow tie)

grated Parmigiano Reggiano cheese (optional)

In a large pot, bring the water to a boil with or without the optional salt.

Place the butter in a large skillet set on medium-high heat and cook until it sizzles, about 2 minutes. Add the shallots and cook for 2 minutes. Add the garlic and salmon and cook 2 minutes more, stirring occasionally to prevent sticking. Pour in the vodka carefully as it may ignite. Add the salt, cream, clam juice and tomato sauce and bring to a boil. Reduce the heat and simmer 5 minutes. Turn off the heat and add the peas.

Cook the pasta in the boiling water according to package directions until just tender. Drain and place it back in the pot. Add the sauce and cook over medium heat, tossing until the pasta is completely coated and most of the sauce is absorbed, about 3 minutes. Sprinkle with the Parmigiano Reggiano cheese, if you wish.

One of my father's few vices was smoking American cigarettes. Unfortunately these were available only on the black market from a dealer called Ciro, the Neapolitan. Ciro smoked continuously, one cigarette after another. His pants were baggy, like two sacks, tied at the waist by an old, cracked black leather belt and his shirt never matched his tie. Nevertheless, he was a charming little devil and even though Father just wanted cigarettes, Ciro would start talking about beautiful and far-away places and by the time he was finished, he would have charmed my father (a consummate salesman himself) into buying other things.

One time we left Ciro's with a package of Norwegian smoked salmon and a bottle of Russian vodka. What followed was a week of intense culinary experimentation: smoked salmon omelette, smoked salmon soufflé, smoked salmon flambé, smoked salmon and anchovy pasta (a memorable disaster). Finally, Father came up with a vodka and smoked salmon sauce. My version of it here always reminds me of Ciro the Neapolitan. God bless him wherever he is.

PASTA WITH SHRIMP AND CAPERS

My brother, Mario, and I thought shrimp and tomato sauce was an unbeatable combination and were always happy when this dish graced our table. If the menu was announced in advance, rest assured that there would be at least a couple of self-invited guests, young and old, also ready to enjoy the bounty.

Occasionally Mother would engage in some sophisticated counter-intelligence, such as innocently forgetting to list the dish on the menu for the nightly meal, which was discussed before anything else at the breakfast table. This ensured a simple family dinner, without unexpected guests. As far as Mario and I were concerned, this was a very favorable outcome, since it meant bigger portions for the two of us!

Serves 4 to 6

INGREDIENTS

3 quarts water (salt optional)
4 tablespoons olive oil
4 garlic cloves, sliced
2 tablespoons chopped shallots
2 teaspoons anchovy paste
1 pound raw shrimp, 21–25 count, shelled and deveined
¼ teaspoon red pepper flakes
½ cup white wine
3 tablespoons capers
¼ teaspoon salt
¼ teaspoon black pepper
3 tablespoons chopped fresh parsley
1 cup clam juice
1 cup Tomato Sauce (see page 137)
1 pound pasta – linguine, spaghetti or spaghettini

In a large stockpot, bring the water to a boil with or without the optional salt.

Put the olive oil, garlic, shallots and anchovy paste into a large sauté pan and cook over medium-high heat until the garlic starts to sizzle, about 2-3 minutes, stirring to mix well. Add the shrimp and red pepper flakes and cook until the shrimp turn pink, about 2 minutes. Pour in the wine and cook for 1 minute. Add all the remaining ingredients except the pasta, bring to a boil for 2 minutes, then reduce the heat and simmer for 1 minute. Turn off the heat.

Cook the pasta in the boiling water according to package directions until just tender. Drain, place it back in the pot and add the sauce, tossing until well coated. Cook for 2 minutes over medium heat or until most of the sauce has been absorbed.

The pasta is now ready to be served. To congratulate yourself, steal a shrimp and enjoy it.

PASTA AL CARTOCCIO DI MARE

SEAFOOD PASTA

Serves 4 to 6

INGREDIENTS

3 quarts water (salt optional)
4 tablespoons olive oil
12 clams, preferably Manila, well scrubbed, in their shells
12 mussels, preferably Penn Cove, bearded and scrubbed, in their shells
4 garlic cloves, sliced
¼ teaspoon red pepper flakes
¼ teaspoon curry powder
12 raw shrimp, shelled and deveined
8 large scallops, cut in half
½ cup cleaned squid, cut in small rings
½ teaspoon salt
½ cup white wine
1 cup Shrimp Stock (see page 141) or clam juice
1 cup Tomato Sauce (see page 137)
2 tablespoons chopped fresh parsley
1 pound pasta – spaghetti, spaghettini or linguine

Preheat the oven to 450° F.

In a large pot, bring the water to a boil with or without the optional salt.

While the water is heating, pour the oil into a large sauté pan set on medium-high heat and cook the clams, mussels, garlic, red pepper and curry powder, covered, for 3 minutes. Add the shrimp, scallops, squid and salt and cook for 2 minutes. Stir in the rest of the ingredients except the pasta, increase the heat to high, bring to a boil, cover and cook for 2 minutes. Remove all the seafood and set aside, with the clams and mussels separated from the shrimp, scallops and squid. Discard any unopened clams or mussels. Reduce the heat to low and continue simmering the sauce, for about 5 minutes.

Cook the pasta in the boiling water until just tender. Drain well, return to the pot and add the simmering sauce and cooked seafood. Toss until well coated, increase the heat to medium and cook for 2 minutes.

CONTINUED ON FOLLOWING PAGE

I love presenting this dish dramatically at the table in its large aluminum packet Once the foil cover is separated, a burst of steam lets a cloud of delectable aroma fill the air. As you continue rolling back the foil to the border of the baking dish, the pasta glistens and shines with the promise of culinary thrills.

I've seen seafood pasta prepared in many ways, but, in my opinion, this is the ultimate version. I'd like to credit my friend Celestino Drago from Drago Restaurant in Santa Monica, California for the idea.

Tear off a large piece of heavy duty, widest-size-possible aluminum foil and lay it out flat on a baking sheet. Spoon the pasta into the middle of the foil and fold both ends over the top. Seal the edges very well and bake in the preheated oven, on the baking sheet, for 5 minutes.

Remove from the oven and slide the foil pouch into a large oval gratin or other serving dish. Bring to the table, cut and roll back the foil for serving in front of your guests. Be careful of the hot steam, but enjoy the beautiful smells and tastes.

COOK'S TIP

If you have the time, you can intensify the flavor of the sauce by increasing the amounts of shrimp stock, wine and tomato sauce by ¼ cup each, and reducing the sauce by one third over high heat after the seafood is removed.

PASTA CON I GAMBERI

PASTA WITH SHRIMP

I'm particularly fond of this seafood pasta dish. Easy, tasty and flavorful, it is the result of much trial and error. From here you can foray into your own more sophisticated culinary medleys.

Serves 4 to 6

INGREDIENTS
3 quarts water (salt optional)
4 tablespoons olive oil
4 garlic cloves, sliced
¾ pound raw shrimp, shelled and deveined
¼ teaspoon red pepper flakes
¾ cup white wine
3 tablespoons chopped fresh parsley
1 cup clam juice or Shrimp Stock (see page 141)
¼ teaspoon salt
1 pound pasta – linguine, spaghettini or spaghetti

In a stockpot, bring the water to a boil with or without the optional salt.

While the pasta water is heating, pour the oil into a large sauté pan set on medium-high heat and sauté the garlic until it starts to sizzle, about 2 minutes. Add the shrimp and red pepper flakes and cook until the shrimp turns pink, about 2 minutes, stirring occasionally to prevent sticking. Add the wine and half the parsley, increase the heat to high and cook for 1 minute. Add the clam juice or shrimp stock and salt, bring to a boil and turn off the heat. The sauce will continue to cook and the flavors will come together.

Cook the pasta according to package directions until just tender. When the pasta is cooked, drain well and return it to the pot. Turn the heat to medium and add the sauce, a little at a time, tossing until the pasta is well coated. Sprinkle with the remaining parsley and stir until most of the sauce has been absorbed, about 2 minutes.

COOK'S TIP
There are many qualities of shrimp on the market and your best selection will depend on where you live. I've had my best success with Mexican shrimp, 20-25 count, which means there are about that many for each pound. I cut them in half when I use them in this recipe to make them bite size. Do not use rock shrimp.

PASTA WITH PEAS, CREAM, AND HAM

In my elementary school years, every child's special days were Christmas and his birthday. Birthdays were elaborate affairs with mothers constantly competing with one another for the coveted best birthday party award. These parties, no matter how elaborate, would live or die by the quality of the food. Of course, my brother and I were both highly respected food critics. Our crushing reviews were the standard by which birthday parties were rated among us kids. The 1965 award belonged to Francesco Maneschi for his Tortellini alla Panna (Tortellini with Cream Sauce). That was the first time I was exposed to pasta with a cream sauce.

What follows is a personal version of this sauce that I've developed over the years at various restaurants. As you'll see, it is a very simple recipe that yields very rich results. I'm sorry to say that there is no way to cut down on its high fat content, therefore, enjoy it in moderation.

Serves 4 to 6

INGREDIENTS

3 quarts water (salt optional)
1½ cups heavy cream
¼ teaspoon salt
3 tablespoons diced baked ham or prosciutto cotto
4 garlic cloves, sliced
3 tablespoons frozen peas
1 pound pasta – tagliatelle, ravioli or tortellini
2 tablespoons grated Parmigiano Reggiano cheese

Bring the water to a boil in a large pot with or without the optional salt.

In a large sauté pan set on medium heat, cook the cream, salt, ham and garlic until the cream comes to a boil, about 4 minutes. Simmer over medium-low heat for 10 minutes until the sauce is thick enough to coat the back of a spoon. Add the peas and cook 2 minutes.

Cook the pasta in the boiling water until just tender. Drain the pasta and return to the pot. Add the warm sauce and toss well over medium-low heat for about 3 minutes. Turn off the heat and top with the Parmigiano Reggiano cheese. Toss well and serve.

COOK'S TIP

If the sauce is cooked too long over high heat, it will separate. If this happens, don't despair. Add a couple of tablespoons of the hot pasta-cooking water. Mix well and voilà – the sauce will come back together in front of your eyes.

PASTA ALLA NANCI

NANCI'S PASTA

Serves 4 to 6

INGREDIENTS

3 quarts water (salt optional)
½ pound Italian sausage
4 tablespoons olive oil
4 garlic cloves, sliced
¼ teaspoon red pepper flakes
2 tablespoons oil-packed sun-dried tomatoes, chopped
1½ pounds fresh tomatoes, peeled and diced
¼ teaspoon salt
1 pound pasta – penne, pennette or rigatoni
2 tablespoons chopped fresh basil

Bring the water to a boil in a large pot with or without the optional salt.

In a small saucepan, bring to a boil just enough water to cover the sausages. Add the sausage links and cook for 5 minutes. Take the sausage out of the hot water and place it in a bowl of cold water to cool. When the sausage is cool enough to handle, dry it with a towel, cut into thin slices and set aside.

Pour the olive oil into a large sauté pan set on medium heat and cook the garlic and red pepper flakes for 3 minutes. Add the sliced sausage and sun-dried tomatoes and cook, tossing well, until the sausage starts to brown, about 3 minutes. Add the diced tomatoes and salt, toss and cook until the sausage is well browned, about 5 minutes. Keep the sauce warm over medium heat.

Cook the pasta in the boiling water according to package directions until just tender. Drain well, return to the pot and add the sauce a little at a time along with the basil, tossing well to coat the pasta with the sauce. Cook on medium heat for 2 minutes.

COOK'S TIP

You don't have to boil the sausage for this recipe. You can use precooked sausages, either pan fried, roasted, or barbecued. My method of parboiling it first makes the sausage a little bit leaner, as most of the fat renders out in the boiling water.

About two months into my first job as head chef at a restaurant, I joined a group of friends for a friendly football game. As usual, I was playing my heart out when a freak accident tore every ligament in my poor beleaguered knee. I realized, lying on the ground, looking up at the sky and trying to forget the intense pain, that I would lose my job.

What followed was surgery and a miserable long stay in the hospital. The pain was terrible, but the food was worse. Multicolored cubes of gelatin were my primary motivation to achieve a level of recovery that would allow me to go home.

On my first night home, my wife prepared the following dish. With the first bite, pain and frustration were part of the past. Life looked hopeful again. I call this dish Pasta alla Nanci and present it to you with the hope that it will unlock the magical powers of your determination, as it did for me.

BAKED PASTA WITH SAUSAGES

My father's cousin was a butcher who had his shop in the town of Alcamo. Knowing my father's maniacal dedication to fresh sausages all'antica (done the old-fashioned way), whenever he was going to be butchering a

pig, he would call us to announce the imminent arrival of the "special sausages." My father's cousin hadn't always been this accommodating, but there was a marked change in his attitude once Father brought him a sample of this famous baked pasta. It became a tradition that, in return for his sausages, we'd provide him with a pan of baked pasta at least twice a year.

Serves 4 to 6

INGREDIENTS

3 quarts water (salt optional)
4 tablespoons olive oil
4 garlic cloves, sliced
1 onion, chopped
⅛ teaspoon red pepper flakes
1 bay leaf
1 pound Italian-style sausage, removed from the casing and crumbled
½ cup red wine
2 cups Beef Stock (see page 140)
2½ cups Tomato Sauce (see page 137)
2 tablespoons chopped fresh basil
1 pound pasta – penne or rigatoni
½ cup grated Romano cheese
3 cups milk
3 tablespoons sweet butter
3 tablespoons all-purpose flour
⅛ teaspoon nutmeg
½ cup grated Parmigiano Reggiano cheese

Bring the water to a boil in a large pot with or without the optional salt.
Pour the olive oil into a large saucepan set on high heat and cook the garlic, onion, red pepper flakes, and bay leaf until the garlic is sizzling, about 2 minutes. Reduce the heat to medium-low, cover and cook, stirring occasionally, for 5 minutes, until the onions are soft. Add the sausage meat, increase the heat to medium-high and cook, stirring well, until the sausage is well browned, about 3 minutes. Add the wine and cook until almost evaporated, stirring well, about 3 minutes. Add the beef stock and tomato sauce and bring to a boil. Reduce the heat to a simmer, add the basil and stir well. Cover with the lid slightly ajar and simmer for 40 minutes, stirring every 10 minutes.

Cook the pasta in the boiling water according to package directions until just tender. When ready, drain well and put it in a large mixing bowl. Pour the sauce on top, add the Romano cheese and mix well. Transfer the pasta to an ovenproof glass baking dish. Preheat the broiler.

Bring the milk to a soft boil in a large saucepan. In another large saucepan, make a roux by combining the butter and flour over medium heat until they form a thick paste. Add the nutmeg to the boiling milk, then pour it a little at a time into the warm roux, whisking vigorously to prevent clumps from forming. When all the milk is added, continue whisking over medium heat until the sauce thickens.

Pour the sauce on top of the pasta and sprinkle with the Parmigiano Reggiano cheese. Place the pasta under the preheated broiler for 3 minutes or until the cheese starts to brown, then bake at 350° F for 10 minutes. Serve immediately.

COOK'S TIP

In my opinion, this baked pasta tastes better the next day. My wife disagrees, therefore we eat half immediately and save the rest for the next day. Reheat it at 350° F for 20 minutes.

PASTA WITH SAUSAGE SAUCE AND RICOTTA

This is a sausage sauce that was popular at our family table and a special treat when fresh ricotta was available. I look back with longing to the days when Father would take me to the shepherd's farm to buy fresh ricotta packaged in traditional cone-shaped wicker baskets, still dripping with whey. We'd always buy at least three baskets since it was a known fact that no matter how hard we tried, we'd end up finishing a whole container all by ourselves before we could make it back home. To this day we still laugh together every time we remember how many of those ricotta baskets we ate together.

Serves 4 to 6

INGREDIENTS

3 cups Tomato Sauce (see page 137)
1 cup Chicken Stock (see page 139)
12 ounces hot Italian sausage, cut into 1-inch-thick rounds
4 garlic cloves, sliced
2 tablespoons chopped fresh basil
1 tablespoon chopped fresh parsley
3 quarts water (salt optional)
1 pound pasta – rigatoni, penne or ziti
6 ounces ricotta cheese
3 tablespoons grated Romano cheese

In a large saucepan, bring the tomato sauce and chicken stock to a soft boil over medium heat. Add the sausage pieces, garlic, basil, and parsley. Bring the sauce back to a soft boil and simmer for 30 minutes, stirring every 10 minutes.

In a large pot, bring the water to a boil with or without the optional salt. Cook the pasta in the boiling water until just tender. Drain the pasta and place back in the pot. Add 1½ cups of the sauce and mix well with a wooden spoon over low heat for about 3 minutes. When the pasta is well coated, add the ricotta and Romano cheeses. Mix well and turn off the heat.

Divide the pasta into individual serving bowls and top with the remaining sauce. Pour yourself a good glass of wine and enjoy your meal!

RISOTTO ALLA MILANESE

RISOTTO WITH SAFFRON

Serves 4 to 6

INGREDIENTS

1½ quarts Chicken Stock (see page 139)
2 tablespoons butter
2 tablespoons olive oil
1 onion, preferably white, finely chopped
2 garlic cloves, chopped
3 cups arborio rice
1 cup white wine
½ teaspoon salt
¼ teaspoon pepper
⅛ teaspoon saffron powder *or* ¼ teaspoon saffron threads
6 tablespoons grated Parmigiano Reggiano cheese

In a large covered pot, bring the chicken stock to a boil, then simmer on the lowest heat.

In a 4-quart saucepan set on medium heat, cook the butter and the olive oil until sizzling, about 2 minutes. Add the onion and cook 2 minutes. Reduce the heat to low, add the garlic and cook for 4 minutes. Add the rice and stir well. Raise the heat to medium-high and add the wine, salt and pepper, cooking until the wine is evaporated, about 2 minutes.

Add 3 cups of the simmering stock and the saffron, stir well, bring to a boil and boil for 2 minutes. Reduce the heat to low, cover the saucepan and let the rice cook undisturbed for 15 minutes. Uncover the saucepan and stir the risotto. Don't worry if it's dry. Raise the heat to medium and add ½ cup of simmering stock, stirring well until it's all incorporated. Continue adding the simmering stock ½ cup at a time and stirring well until the risotto is cooked. This process will take about 5-8 minutes. Taste the rice with each addition of stock. The rice is perfectly cooked when it is tender to the bite. Don't worry if there is additional stock left.

Turn off the heat, add a final ½ cup of stock and the grated cheese, mix well and let it rest for 3 minutes. Stir well and serve while still piping hot.

There are two schools of thought when it comes to risotto. One advocates the perfect consistency as "asciutto" (dry), which is a creamy, porridge-like consistency. The other advocates "all'onda" as the ultimate and only style, which is very liquid with the consistency of a thick soup.

To me, what matters first is the flavor. In the following recipes, I've developed a very simple, almost foolproof technique that will take away any fear you might have about attempting the preparation of this Italian culinary masterpiece. Trust me; with a little bit of practice, you will never again be afraid to compare your risotto with any other version available, even those of the best restaurants.

Please, do not assume that all the simmering stock has to be used. The quantities will differ depending on the heat you use throughout the cooking and how long the stock has been boiling. With some experience, you'll be able to gauge the perfect timing for everything. Ultimately, you'll decide what school of thought you belong to – asciutto or all'onda.

The sauce for this risotto is based on balsamic vinegar, and I think you'll be surprised by its incredible tangy, sweet-and-sour flavor. I'm so taken by it that I often use it for other risotto variations.

RISOTTO ALLA MODENESE

RISOTTO WITH BALSAMIC SAUCE

Serves 4 to 6

INGREDIENTS

1½ quarts Chicken Stock (see page 139)
2 tablespoons butter
2 tablespoons olive oil
1 onion, preferably white, finely chopped
2 garlic cloves, chopped
3 cups arborio rice
1 cup white wine
½ teaspoon salt
¼ teaspoon pepper
½ cup heavy cream (optional)
3 tablespoons chopped fresh Italian parsley
6 tablespoons grated Parmigiano Reggiano cheese

SAUCE:

1 cup balsamic vinegar
4 garlic cloves, sliced
4 (2-inch) pieces fresh rosemary
2 tablespoons butter (optional)

In a covered 2-quart stockpot, bring the stock to a boil then simmer on the lowest heat.

In a 4-quart saucepan, cook the butter and the olive oil over medium heat until sizzling, about 2 minutes. Add the onion, stir well and cook for 3 more minutes. Reduce the heat to low, add the garlic and cook for 4 minutes. Add the rice, stir well, raise the heat to medium-high and add the wine, salt and pepper, stirring continuously until all the liquid has evaporated, about 2 minutes.

Add 3 cups of the simmering stock and bring to a boil, stirring continuously. Reduce the heat to a low simmer, cover the saucepan and cook 15 minutes undisturbed.

SAUCE:

While the rice simmers, prepare the sauce. Put all the sauce ingredients except the butter into a nonstick saucepan and bring to a boil. Reduce the heat and simmer until it reduces by half, about 10 minutes. The sauce is ready when it coats the back of a spoon. For those of you with decadent attitudes toward the richness of sauces, add the optional butter and stir well. Set aside while you finish the risotto.

Stir the risotto. Don't worry if it is dry. Raise the heat to medium and add ½ cup of the remaining simmering stock, stirring until it's all incorporated. Continue adding the simmering stock ½ cup at a time and stirring until the risotto is cooked. This process will take about 5-8 minutes. Taste the rice with each addition of stock. It is perfectly cooked when tender to the bite. Don't worry if there is additional stock left.

Turn off the heat, add the optional cream or ½ cup of the remaining simmering stock, the parsley and the cheese. Mix well and let rest for about 3 minutes.

Serve the risotto in deep pasta bowls and top each serving with no more than 1½ tablespoons of the sauce. (Discard the garlic and rosemary before serving the sauce.)

I've confessed to you my fondness for wild mushrooms, especially porcini, in previous recipes. Well, my dear friends, get ready, because I'm about to introduce you to the best recipe ever developed for a wild mushroom risotto.

Serves 4 to 6

INGREDIENTS

1½ quarts Chicken Stock (see page 139)
2 tablespoons butter
2 tablespoons olive oil
1 onion, preferably white, finely chopped
3 garlic cloves, chopped
¼ cup fresh or fresh-frozen porcini mushrooms, thinly sliced, *or* ½ ounce dried, broken into small pieces
½ cup fresh crimini or portobello mushrooms, thinly sliced
½ cup fresh shiitake mushrooms, stems removed, thinly sliced
3 tablespoons chopped fresh parsley
1½ cups white wine
3 cups arborio rice
¾ teaspoon salt
¼ teaspoon pepper
½ cup heavy cream (optional)
3 tablespoons butter (optional)
5 tablespoons grated Parmigiano Reggiano cheese

In a covered 2-quart stockpot, bring the stock to a boil then reduce the heat to low and simmer.

In a 4-quart saucepan set on medium heat, cook the 2 tablespoons of butter and the olive oil until sizzling, about 2 minutes. Add the onion, stir well and cook 2 minutes. Reduce the heat to low, add the garlic, stir well and cook 4 minutes. Raise the heat to medium-high, add the mushrooms and 1 tablespoon of the parsley and cook for 3 minutes, stirring to prevent sticking. Add the wine and deglaze the saucepan. Make sure you dislodge all the brown bits that might stick to the bottom of the pan. Cook for 2 minutes. Add the rice, salt and pepper and stir continuously until all of the wine has evaporated, about 2 minutes.

Add 3 cups of the simmering stock and bring to a boil, stirring continuously for 2 minutes. Reduce the heat to a low simmer, cover the saucepan and let the rice cook 15 minutes undisturbed.

Stir the risotto. Don't worry if it is dry. Raise the heat to medium and add ½ cup of simmering stock, stirring well until it is all incorporated. Continue adding the simmering stock ½ cup at a time and stirring well until the risotto is cooked. This process will take about 5-8 minutes. Taste the rice with each addition of stock. It is perfectly cooked when tender to the bite. Don't worry if you haven't used all of the simmering stock.

Turn off the heat, add the optional cream and butter if you wish, the rest of the parsley, the cheese and ½ cup of remaining simmering stock. Mix well and let the risotto rest for 3 minutes.

Serve in deep pasta bowls, making sure you give yourself the biggest helping – after all, you did all this cooking and deserve it. On the other hand, if you want to impress somebody, give him or her the biggest helping. Be aware that such acts of generosity are often short lived and you'll soon go back to giving yourself the biggest helping.

COOK'S TIP

In case you can't find fresh porcini mushrooms, you can use dried – about ½–¾ ounce. Soften them in 2 cups of hot stock for about 20 minutes. Chop them up and add them to the other mushrooms. Strain the leftover soaking stock into the risotto as part of the initial 3 cups of liquid.

SAUSAGE AND SUN-DRIED TOMATO RISOTTO

Once you understand the basics of risotto-making, there is no limit to what you can do. This recipe was originally developed as an alternative to home delivery pizza. (Yes, I confess I do sometimes take comfort in the practical simplicity of a delivered pizza.) Anyway, in this particular instance I made a heroic recovery from my attack of laziness. In a last minute desperate effort, I raided the refrigerator for a final attempt to prepare a wholesome home-cooked meal. This recipe is the glorious result. What started as an act of cowardly resignation turned into a magnificent culinary feast.

Serves 4 to 6

INGREDIENTS

1½ quarts Chicken Stock (see page 139)
2 tablespoons butter
2 tablespoons olive oil
1 small red onion, chopped
3 garlic cloves, chopped
4 tablespoons oil-packed sun-dried tomatoes, chopped
10 ounces hot Italian sausage, thinly sliced
⅛ teaspoon red pepper flakes
2 tablespoons chopped fresh basil
2 tablespoons chopped fresh parsley
1½ cups red wine
3 cups arborio rice
¾ teaspoon salt
¼ teaspoon black pepper
2 tablespoons grated Romano cheese
2 tablespoons grated Parmigiano Reggiano cheese
3 tablespoons butter (optional)

In a covered 2-quart pot, bring the stock to a boil, reduce the heat to low and let simmer.

In a 4-quart saucepan set on medium heat, cook the 2 tablespoons of butter and the olive oil until sizzling, about 2 minutes. Add the onion, stir well and cook 2 minutes. Reduce the heat to low, add the garlic, stir well and cook for 4 minutes. Raise the heat to medium, add the sun-dried tomatoes, sausage, red pepper flakes, 1 tablespoon of the basil and 1 tablespoon of the parsley and cook 3 minutes, stirring to prevent sticking. Add the red wine and deglaze the saucepan. Make sure you dislodge all the brown bits that might cling to the bottom and cook for 2 minutes. Add the rice, salt and pepper, stirring continuously until all the wine has evaporated, about 2 minutes.

Add 3 cups of the simmering stock and bring to a boil while stirring continuously. Reduce the heat to a low simmer, cover and let cook undisturbed for 15 minutes.

Stir the risotto. Don't worry if it is dry. Raise the heat to medium, add ½ cup of the remaining simmering stock, stirring continuously until it is all incorporated. Continue adding the simmering stock ½ cup at a time, stirring continuously until the risotto is cooked. This process will take about 5-8 minutes. Taste the rice with each addition of stock. It is perfectly cooked when tender to the bite. Don't worry if you haven't used up all the simmering stock.

Turn off the heat, add ½ cup of the remaining simmering stock, the cheeses, the remaining basil, the remaining parsley and the optional butter if you wish. Mix well and let the risotto rest for 2 more minutes.

Distribute into deep pasta bowls and bring it to the table.

COOK'S TIP

The best way to cut paper-thin slices of sausage is to freeze it first and then slice with a serrated knife.

I SECONDI

Entrees

POLLO ARROSTO AL VINO

ROASTED CHICKEN WITH HERBS AND WINE

Serves 4

INGREDIENTS

1 (4-pound) chicken, washed and patted dried

2 cups white wine

2 tablespoons chopped garlic

¾ teaspoon salt

¾ teaspoon pepper

1 tablespoon chopped fresh rosemary

1 tablespoon chopped fresh sage

2 tablespoons olive oil

SAUCE:

2 tablespoons chicken fat, spooned from the cooking juices

1 tablespoon finely chopped onion

⅔ cup reduced wine marinade

¼ cup defatted chicken roasting juices

¾ cup Chicken Stock (see page 139)

1½ teaspoons cornstarch

⅛ teaspoon salt (optional)

1 teaspoon chopped fresh sage

Chicken is what you make of it. In our family, cooking chicken became a mission and between my grandmother and my father, roasted chicken was elevated to an artistic endeavor with spiritual undertones.

What follows is a very simple recipe which will never betray you and displays the great potential of this common bird. Remember to start the night before with the marinade step. Try it with my Country-Style Roasted Potatoes (see page 114) for a match made in heaven.

Marinate the chicken overnight in the white wine, turning at least once, in the refrigerator.

Preheat the oven to 425° F. Place the garlic, salt, pepper, rosemary and sage on a chopping board and, with a sharp knife, chop and blend them together. Do not do this in a blender as it will ruin the texture. Chop the mixture as fine as you can.

Take the chicken out of the marinade, reserving the marinade for the sauce. Dry the chicken well with paper towels. Loosen the skin, pushing with your fingers around the breast, thighs and back. Stuff ⅔ of the chopped seasoning mixture underneath the skin over the thighs, legs, breast, and back. Place the chicken on a vertical roaster, brush it with the olive oil and rub the remaining herb mixture over the skin.

Reduce the oven temperature to 350° F. Roast the chicken in the preheated oven for 30 minutes. Remove from the oven, turn the chicken

CONTINUED ON FOLLOWING PAGE

¼ turn clockwise and brush it well with the juices that have accumulated in the bottom of the pan. Cover the top part of the chicken with a piece of foil just up to the wings to keep it from getting too brown. Roast for 1 more hour, repeating the turning and basting every 30 minutes. Test the chicken to see if it's fully cooked by inserting the tip of a sharp knife in the thickest part of the thigh. If it's fully cooked, the juices that run out will be clear. If they're not completely clear, cook 10 more minutes. Remove the chicken from the oven and let it rest for 10 minutes.

While the chicken is cooking, pour the marinade into a saucepan. Cook over high heat until reduced by ⅔. Remove from the heat and set aside.

When the chicken is done, remove it from the vertical roaster, taking care not to spill the juices that have accumulated in the pan. Cut it into serving pieces as you wish. Place the pieces on a warm serving platter and keep warm while you make the sauce.

SAUCE:

Pour the cooking juices into a defatting cup, reserving 2 tablespoons fat. In a small nonstick sauté pan on medium heat, cook the chicken fat and onion for 3 minutes. Add the reduced marinade and cook for 1 minute. Add the defatted roasting juices and ½ cup of the chicken stock and bring to a boil. In a cup, mix the remaining ¼ cup of chicken stock with the cornstarch and stir into the boiling sauce, stirring well until the sauce thickens, about 1 minute. Reduce the heat to a simmer, taste for salt, adding the additional ⅛ teaspoon if you wish, and the sage for added flavor.

When you're ready to serve, pour the juices from the serving platter into the simmering sauce and serve it in a gravy boat alongside the chicken.

COOK'S TIP

If you don't have a vertical roaster, you can roast the chicken in a more traditional way. Start with the chicken, breast-side-up, for the first 30 minutes. Turn it over onto its other breast-side and cook for 15 minutes. Turn on each thigh-side and its back for 15 minutes each and finish with a breast-side-up, for the last 15 minutes. Remember to baste the chicken at every turn. The chicken will be wobbly as you balance it on its different body parts; just balance it as best you can against the pan.

A G G L A S S A T U

O N I O N   G L A Z E D   P O T   R O A S T

Serves 4 to 6

INGREDIENTS

1 (2½-3 pound) boneless beef chuck roast, tied
3 teaspoons salt
¾ teaspoon black pepper
2 tablespoons all-purpose flour
4 tablespoons olive oil
3 tablespoons butter
3 pounds onions, peeled and sliced
3 bay leaves
6 garlic cloves, sliced
¼ teaspoon red pepper flakes
¼ teaspoon dried thyme
2½ cups white wine
¾ cup Marsala wine
6¼ cups Chicken Stock (see page 139)

Agglassatu is a remarkable example of how a common cut of meat, when combined with a few other common, uncomplicated ingredients, reaches a level of uncommon distinction. In Palermo, each family's pot roast recipe is a jealously guarded treasure passed on ceremonially from mother to daughter. My mother's version was a favorite dish in my home. She always made a great deal of sauce so there would be enough to top the pasta serving that preceded the main entree.

Sprinkle the roast with 1 teaspoon of the salt, the pepper and the flour, shaking off the excess flour. In a large nonstick sauté pan set on medium heat, cook 1½ tablespoons of the olive oil until very hot, about 2 minutes. When the oil is hot, brown the meat on all sides, about 3 minutes. Transfer the browned roast to a large bowl and set aside.

In a large stockpot or Dutch oven set on medium heat, cook the remaining olive oil and butter until the butter melts and the oil is hot, about 2 minutes. Add the onions, bay leaves, garlic, red pepper flakes, thyme and 1 teaspoon of the salt and cook, stirring occasionally, until the onions are soft, about 5 minutes. Add the white wine and Marsala, increase the heat to high and bring to a boil, stirring frequently. Cook until reduced by half, about 5-8 minutes.

Add the browned meat and the juices that have accumulated in the bowl, the chicken stock, and the remaining salt and bring to a boil. Reduce the heat to low, cover and simmer for 2 hours, turning the meat once every ½ hour.

CONTINUED ON FOLLOWING PAGE

Transfer the meat to a carving board to rest. Increase the heat to high, bring the sauce to a boil, stirring frequently, and cook until reduced by half, about 30-40 minutes. It should be light brown in color and quite thick, like heavy cream.

Cut the meat into thin slices. Remove half of the sauce, about 2½ cups, from the pot and save it as a sauce for pasta, if you wish. Transfer the sliced meat to the remaining sauce and reheat gently. Serve on a large platter with mashed potatoes and the sauce on the side.

COOK'S TIP

If by the time you reach the sauce consistency you want, there isn't enough for both the meat and pasta, add enough additional stock to make 2½ cups of sauce for the meat and 1½ cups for the pasta.

FALSO MAGRO

STUFFED MEAT ROLLS

Serves 8 to 10

INGREDIENTS

1½ pounds Italian sausage, removed from the casings

1 egg

½ cup plain bread crumbs

¼ cup grated Parmigiano Reggiano cheese

2 large slices top round beef, cut ¼ inch thick (about 1½ pounds and approximately 5 x 11 inches each)

6 large slices mortadella or bologna (about ½ pound)

5 hard-boiled eggs

¼ pound imported provola piccante (sharp provolone), cut into long sticks

¼ pound soppressata-style salami, thinly sliced

¼ cup olive oil

½ cup all-purpose flour

2 garlic cloves, peeled and left whole

1 onion, finely chopped

1 carrot, finely chopped

1 rib celery, finely chopped

¾ cup red wine

3 cups Beef Stock (see page 140)

2 bay leaves

4⅓ cups Tomato Sauce (see page 137)

Holiday preparations are much the same in Italy as in America. Decorated homes, freshly cut pine trees, the fragrance of roasting chestnuts and beautiful store windows abound in both countries. The food traditions, however, are worlds apart.

My mother's style of holiday fare combined the traditions of the Veneto region and Sicily. The holidays were her opportunity to shine and she borrowed freely from both cuisines to create menus that rarely featured the same dishes two years in a row.

The dish that follows is typically Sicilian, in the "stile baronale" (the baronial style), which means the most sophisticated and wildly rich of all styles. The flavors will attack your palate from the firs bite and then pummel you into a passive state of "gourmande" bliss!

The day before serving, preheat the oven to 400° F.

Mix the sausage with the raw egg, bread crumbs, and cheese, kneading well to incorporate all the ingredients. Pound the meat slices lightly, being careful not to tear the meat. Place the slices next to each other on a cutting board, slightly overlapping. Top the meat with 3 slices of the mortadella. Place half the sausage mixture down the middle, spreading the mixture to within 1 inch of the edges. Place the hard-boiled eggs end-to-end on the center. Top with the provolone, salami and the remaining sausage mixture. Lift the long side of the meat roll over the stuffing and roll tightly to form a long sausage shape 10 inches long. The roll may tear and let some of the filling spill out.

CONTINUED ON FOLLOWING PAGE

Don't worry. Patch the holes with salami slices. Use toothpicks to secure the roll's edges and tie it securely with kitchen twine. Tie a loop around the roll at one end and secure it with a double knot. Cut the string and tie another loop 2 inches from the first. Continue tying loops around the roll until you have reached the other end. Now take a long piece of string and tie it to a loop at one end of the roll. Without cutting the string, tie it to each of the loops along one side of the roll, turn the roll over and repeat this on the other side with the same piece of string. The final knot should be secured to the original loop. The toothpicks can now be removed.

Heat the oil in a large nonstick sauté pan, until sizzling. Dust the roll with flour and sear it on all sides, 2 minutes on a side. Remove from the pan and set aside.

Using the oil left in the pan, sauté the garlic, onion, carrot and celery over medium heat, until soft, 5 minutes. Deglaze the pan with the wine and reduce it by half, about 10-12 minutes. Pour the mixture into a blender, add 1 cup of the beef stock and process until smooth. Pour the mixture into a roasting pan, add the bay leaves, the meat, 1 cup of the beef stock and the tomato sauce. Place in the oven, reduce the heat to 325° F, and cook for 1 hour, turning and basting the meat with the sauce every 20 minutes. Remove from the oven, cool to room temperature, cover and refrigerate overnight.

The next day, cut the twine and slice the meat into ¼- to ½-inch slices. Place the slices in a large sauté pan, cover with the sauce and the remaining 1 cup of the beef stock. Reheat gently until heated through. Place in the middle of a large platter with the slices overlapping and top with your beautiful sauce. I'd suggest serving this dish with the Peas with Onion and Bacon (see page 108) and the Garlic Mashed Potatoes (see page 112).

SALSICCIE BRASATE CON I RAPINI

BRAISED SAUSAGE WITH BROCCOLI RAPE

Serves 4 to 6

INGREDIENTS
4 teaspoons olive oil
4 garlic cloves, sliced
1 onion, chopped
¼ teaspoon red pepper flakes
1 (1-pound) bunch broccoli rape or mustard greens, cut into 1-inch pieces
1½ cups Chicken Stock (see page 139)
2 cups Tomato Sauce (see page 137)
1 pound sweet Italian sausage (about 6-8 links)

In a 10-inch sauté pan set on medium heat, cook the oil, garlic, onion and red pepper flakes until the onion is soft, about 5 minutes. Add the broccoli rape or greens, toss until well coated with the oil, and cook for 3 minutes. Pour in the chicken stock and tomato sauce and bring to a boil. Prick small holes in the casing of each individual sausage link with a fork and add to the sauce. Reduce the heat to medium-low, cover with the lid halfway off, and cook for 40 minutes, stirring occasionally. Remove the lid and cook for 15 minutes more. Transfer to a long oval serving dish and bring to the table.

COOK'S TIP
If the sauce is too watery because of the water released by the vegetables, remove the sausages once they're cooked through, and reduce the sauce over medium-high heat until it reaches your desired consistency. Return the sausages to the sauce, heat through and serve.

Mother discovered early in her cooking career that to appease the finicky taste of Mario and me when it came to vegetables, she would have to use creative culinary disguises.

The following recipe is a perfect example of her devious, yet fabulous, cooking. The broccoli rape coupled with the sausage is a country-style gourmet dish. It's delicious with a side of my Garlic Mashed Potatoes (see page 112) and plenty of country-style Italian bread.

Mustard greens can be substituted for the broccoli rape.

LAMB CHOPS WITH ENZINO'S PESTO

Every time I prepare this dish I think of summer nights at my grandmother's country house. I remember the smell of barbecued meats, the brilliance of the fresh young wines, the laughter and the beautiful feeling of our family sharing a delightful meal together.

What follows is the recipe for my father's special barbecued lamb chops and pesto-style sauce.

"Pesto," in this case refers to the grinding of the sauce ingredients with a mortar and pestle. For those of you without this useful tool, I suggest an alternative method in the recipe.

Serves 4

INGREDIENTS
1 (1-pound) can peeled Italian tomatoes
2½ tablespoons chopped garlic
1 tablespoon chopped fresh rosemary
1¾ teaspoons salt
¾ teaspoon pepper
¼ cup olive oil
2½ teaspoons chopped fresh mint
1 (2-pound) rack of lamb, trimmed by a butcher and cut into 9 chops

The day before serving drain the tomatoes and break them up, reserving the juices.

With a large mortar and pestle, grind the garlic, rosemary, salt and pepper into a paste. Add the tomatoes and grind them into the paste. You'll do this by moving the pestle slowly and forcefully from side to side while grinding the ingredients to a homogenous red paste.

Put the paste in a large bowl and add the reserved tomato juices, the oil and mint and whisk until it has the consistency of a loose salad dressing. Let it rest for 10 minutes and it is ready to use.

If you don't have a mortar and pestle in your kitchen, let me provide you with an alternative method to effectively prepare Enzino's Pesto. Smash the garlic cloves to a pulp using the bottom of a clean saucepan. Put the crushed garlic in a wooden salad bowl and add the salt and pepper. Using the back of a large wooden spoon, mash the garlic against the side of the bowl, incorporating the rosemary, salt and pepper until it becomes an homogenous pulp. If you do not have a wooden salad bowl, improvise by using the flat surface of a wood chopping board. Place the garlic mixture in a steel bowl and continue with the rest of the recipe.

Place the lamb chops in a dish with the pesto sauce, cover and marinate in the refrigerator overnight, turning at least once.

Just before cooking, remove the chops from the marinade, reserving the marinade separately. Barbecue the lamb chops over a hot charcoal grill or cook under a broiler, 3-5 minutes per side, basting frequently with the leftover reserved marinade. When the lamb is ready, keep it warm while you pour the leftover marinade into a pan and bring it to a boil. Boil for 3 minutes, pour it into a sauceboat and serve alongside the lamb.

COOK'S TIP

For extra fragrance, use 2 thick rosemary branches, 7 to 10 inches long, tied together as your basting tool. This will not be a primary flavoring agent for the lamb, but will greatly enhance your own cooking pleasure ... I can almost smell the aroma now!

You can also use this pesto as a pasta sauce. Simply reduce the garlic to 1 tablespoon and the salt to 1 teaspoon. Toss 1½ cups of the pesto with 1 pound of cooked pasta and sprinkle with your choice of grated cheese.

For summer barbecues at my grandmother's country house near Alcamo, the kids would be dispatched out to the vineyards or down to the barn, where there were always large piles of dry grapevine branches. We would run back like ferrets, our arms full of vines, racing for first place. The men would build the fire and by noon time it would be reduced to the orange glow of hot charcoals.

While waiting for the coals to be ready, we played in the fields, fighting imaginary battles. The men stood around minding the fire and drinking last year's wine while looking ahead to the current vintage, swapping opinions about sports, politics, work and taxes. The women pulled together the ingredients for the lunch meal in the kitchen, talking about their families while keeping an eye on the roving pack of wild young rascals running freely through the vineyards.

Serves 4

INGREDIENTS
4 (8-10 ounce) pork chops, cut 1½ inches thick
salt and pepper to taste
1 recipe Stuffing (either Vegetarian on page 118 or Sausage on page 119)
2 tablespoons olive oil
2 cups Chicken Stock (see page 139)
2 garlic cloves, sliced
1¼ teaspoons cornstarch
½ teaspoon chopped fresh parsley

Preheat the oven to 475° F.

Cut a pocket along one side of each pork chop and salt and pepper the inside of the pocket. Fill the pocket with the stuffing of your choice. Salt and pepper both sides of the chops.

Pour the olive oil into a nonstick sauté pan with an ovenproof handle and cook over high heat until the oil is sizzling. Add the stuffed chops and cook 2 minutes per side until well browned. Remove the chops to a serving dish. Discard the fat from the pan, add 1¾ cups of the chicken stock and the garlic and bring to a boil over high heat, 2 minutes. Add the chops, cover and place in the preheated oven for 12 minutes.

Mix the remaining ¼ cup stock with the cornstarch.

When the chops are cooked, place them on a serving dish and cover with a tent of aluminum foil to keep them warm. (Be careful when removing the pan from the oven – the pan handle will be very hot!)

Bring the stock remaining in the pan to a boil. Add the parsley, ¼ teaspoon salt, ⅛ teaspoon pepper, and the cornstarch mixture, stirring constantly until the sauce thickens, about 2 minutes. Return the chops and their accumulated juices to the pan and reheat for 3 minutes over medium heat.

Transfer the chops back to the serving dish, top with the sauce and serve with Garlic Mashed Potatoes (see page 112) and Sweet and Sour Pearl Onions (see page 107).

COOK'S TIP

The cooking times given are for a slightly pink pork chop that is very tender. Increase the cooking time if you want yours well done.

From time to time, these images unexpectedly creep into my mind and I can feel them as vividly as if I were still there. But most of all, I remember huge quantities of grilled chops, baked artichokes, marinated eggplants, roasted peppers, sliced dry salami, farm ricotta still dripping and rounds of pecorino cheese covered with pepper. It was all served on chipped china dishes with delicate flower motifs. The table was decorated with a multitude of china and silverware patterns on a long white tablecloth. My grandmother would sit at the head of the table and lunch would begin.

What follows is one of my favorite dishes from these family get-togethers, but my recipe will allow you to cook it all year round instead of just at summer barbecues. I hope you, too, will make beautiful memories with it.

CONTROFILETTO DI MAIALE RIPIENO

GRILLED PORK TENDERLOIN WITH PROSCIUTTO AND PROVOLONE

Mentioning this recipe always brings on a longing for times gone by. I see the smiles of familiar faces and hear their heartfelt laughter as the summer wind brushes my skin. The sun rolls behind the hills and the hot coals

of the barbecue glow as evening approaches. Aromas of grilling meats float in the air.

I invite you to enjoy this recipe with your special friends al fresco, out in the open air. But don't rush. Sit back and savor the special moments that will unfold as this old, enchanted recipe from my family works its magic on you.

Serves 4

INGREDIENTS

4 (6-ounce) pieces pork tenderloin, each about 5 inches long
3 ounces prosciutto, finely diced
3 ounces provolone cheese, finely diced
2 tablespoons olive oil
1½ tablespoons chopped garlic
1½ tablespoons chopped fresh rosemary
¼ teaspoon salt
⅛ teaspoon pepper

Make sure you remove all of the membrane that covers the pork. Make a lengthwise slit in the middle of each piece with a long, thin-bladed knife.

Mix the prosciutto and provolone pieces in a small bowl. Stuff the slit of the tenderloin pieces with this mixture, pressing well with your fingers. Brush the stuffed pieces with 1 tablespoon of the oil and roll them in the chopped garlic and rosemary until well coated. Wrap with plastic wrap and refrigerate for a few hours to allow the flavors to penetrate the meat.

Light the barbecue and wait until the coals stop flaming and turn red hot. Arrange a grill rack at least 3 inches away from the coals.

Brush the stuffed pork pieces with the remaining 1 tablespoon of the oil and sprinkle with the salt and pepper. Cook the meat on the barbecue until it reaches your desired doneness, about 8-10 minutes on each side. Let them rest on a heated platter for a few minutes, then serve.

COOK'S TIP

The cooking time on the barbecue will always vary depending on the type of wood or coals you use. After cooking 5 minutes on each side, cut into a piece to visually check the doneness. I prefer my meat just slightly pink.

B R A I S E D   V E A L   S H A N K S

Serves 6

INGREDIENTS

1 teaspoon salt
1 teaspoon pepper
6 (8-10 ounce) veal shanks, 1½-2 inches thick
¼ cup all-purpose flour
6 tablespoons olive oil
1 cup white wine
1 carrot, finely chopped
1 onion, finely chopped
1 rib celery, finely chopped
4 ounces shiitake or white button mushrooms, diced
4 whole garlic cloves
2 whole cloves
2 bay leaves
2 cups Tomato Sauce (see page 137)
2 cups Beef or Chicken Stock (see page 139-140)
¼ cup dried porcini mushrooms, broken into small pieces

Preheat the oven to 375° F.

Salt and pepper the veal shanks and dust with the flour, shaking well to remove the excess.

Heat 3 tablespoons of the oil in a large sauté pan set on high heat until sizzling. Add the veal shanks and cook for 2 minutes on each side until well browned. Transfer the shanks to a 9 x 13-inch ovenproof casserole. Deglaze the pan with ½ cup of the wine, stirring well with a wooden spoon to dislodge any brown bits from the bottom. Cook until the wine is reduced by half, 3-5 minutes, and pour over the meat in the casserole.

CONTINUED ON FOLLOWING PAGE

*T*his dish lives as a milestone in Italian culinary history, the secret of its preparation kept a closely guarded culinary secret. Famous chefs have been known to sneak in their secret ingredients away from the watching eyes of their assistants. In breaking with tradition, I would like to share my personal version of Ossobuco, a foolproof recipe that will yield nothing short of sensational results.

Wipe the sauté pan clean with a paper towel. Heat the remaining 3 tablespoons of olive oil in the pan over high heat for 2 minutes, until sizzling. Add the carrot, onion, celery, mushrooms, garlic, cloves and bay leaves and cook for 2 minutes, stirring well. Reduce the heat to medium-low and cook 5 minutes. Raise the heat to medium-high and deglaze the pan with the remaining ½ cup of white wine, cooking until the wine is reduced by half, stirring well. Add the tomato sauce, stock and the porcini mushrooms and bring to a boil, stirring well. Pour over the meat in the casserole. Cover the casserole loosely with heavy duty foil. Put in the preheated oven, reduce the heat to 350° F and cook for 1½ hours. Remove the foil and cook 1 hour more, turning the meat once. Test the meat for doneness. If you're using 2-inch-thick pieces, add 10 more minutes. The sauce should be very rich and tasty. Adjust the salt to your taste. Serve this dish with Garlic Mashed Potatoes (see page 112) or Risotto with Saffron (see page 55).

COOK'S TIPS

I'd suggest tying the meat with kitchen twine to help keep its shape while braising in the oven.

You will achieve a smoother sauce by processing the raw carrots, onions and celery in the food processor for about 1 minute.

SALTIMBOCCA

VEAL WITH SAGE AND PROSCIUTTO

Serves 4

INGREDIENTS

1 pound veal scaloppine, pounded thin
¼ pound prosciutto ham, thinly sliced
20 fresh sage leaves
¼ teaspoon salt
1½ tablespoons vegetable oil
3 tablespoons butter, softened
½ cup white wine or Marsala
1 cup Chicken or Beef Stock (see pages 139-140)
⅛ teaspoon pepper
½ tablespoon all-purpose flour

Veal scaloppine are as popular on an Italian menu as a dish of pasta. It was a common entree at our table, especially in summer, when we spent so much time at the beach that Mother wanted quick-fix dishes like this one for lunch.

Veal is a very versatile cut of meat and can be prepared in many different ways. This recipe will give you great results and you'll be amazed at how much flavor the ingredients provide. You must use Italian or Italian-style prosciutto. No substitute will do! Also, fresh sage is a must.

Cut the veal into 3 x 4-inch pieces. Place a slice of prosciutto on top of each piece of veal and top with a leaf of fresh sage. Skewer with a toothpick to hold the three together and sprinkle the bottom sides with ⅛ teaspoon of the salt.

Pour the oil and 1 tablespoon of the butter into a large sauté pan and cook over high heat until almost smoking. Add the veal slices and sauté 30 seconds on each side, shaking the pan to prevent sticking. Transfer the veal to another dish and pour the oil out of the pan. Place the pan back on the heat and deglaze with the wine, cooking until reduced to a thick glaze, about 2 minutes. Pour in the stock and the remaining salt and the pepper, and bring to a boil. Reduce the heat to a simmer, return the meat to the pan and cook for 2 minutes.

While the meat is heating, mix the remaining soft butter with the flour to make a thick paste. Remove the meat from the pan and place on a serving dish. Bring the stock to a boil and add the butter/flour paste, one spoonful at a time, whisking well until the sauce is thick. Pour it over the meat and serve.

COOK'S TIP

If you'd like more sauce, increase the wine by 2 tablespoons, the stock by ¼ cup, and the flour/butter mix by 1 teaspoon of flour.

VEAL SCALOPPINE WITH CAPERS AND LEMON

This is a very simple main dish that will make you look like a world-class chef. Veal scaloppine are very versatile and easily available in supermarkets. The key element in the preparation of this recipe is not to overcook the veal, as it is cut very thin and will take less than a minute per side.

Serves 4

INGREDIENTS

1 pound veal scaloppine
¼ teaspoon salt
¼ teaspoon pepper
4 tablespoons flour
3 tablespoons vegetable oil
4 tablespoons butter
½ cup white wine
4 tablespoons drained capers
2 tablespoons lemon juice
1¼ cups Chicken Stock (see page 139)

Pound the veal slices lightly, sprinkle with salt and pepper and dust with flour. Pour the oil and 1 tablespoon of the butter into a large nonstick sauté pan and cook over medium heat until the oil starts to sizzle. The oil must be hot in order to seal the meat's juices in. Add the veal slices and cook 30 seconds on each side. Don't cook any longer or the veal will be tough. Remove the veal from the pan and pour off the oil.

Place the pan on high heat, deglaze with the wine and reduce by half, 4-5 minutes. Add the capers, lemon juice and chicken stock and bring to a boil for 2 minutes. Return the meat to the pan and reheat it in the sauce for 1 minute. Transfer the meat to a serving platter. Add the remaining butter to the sauce, turn off the heat, and stir to incorporate the butter. Pour the hot sauce over the veal and serve.

COOK'S TIP

For a thicker sauce, soften the 3 tablespoons of butter and combine it with 1½ tablespoons of the flour used to dust the meat. In the last step, do not turn off the heat when you add the butter/flour mixture. Stir well with a wooden spoon for 1 to 2 minutes, until the sauce thickens. Add 2 teaspoons of chopped parsley for a bit of color.

The thickness of the sauce will be determined by the amount of the flour/butter mixture you use.

SPEZZATINO DELLA NONNA

GRANDMA'S VEAL STEW

Serves 4 to 5

INGREDIENTS

1½ pounds veal stewing meat, cut into 1-inch cubes
¾ teaspoon salt
½ teaspoon pepper
1½ tablespoons all-purpose flour
3 tablespoons olive oil
1 small carrot, finely chopped
1 onion, finely chopped
4 garlic cloves, sliced
1 rib celery, finely chopped
1 tablespoon chopped fresh rosemary
1 tablespoon chopped fresh basil
2 bay leaves
1 cup white wine
1 (1-pound) can peeled Italian tomatoes
1 cup Chicken Stock (see page 139)
½ pound potatoes, peeled and cut into 1½-inch cubes
½ pound carrots, cut into ½-inch cubes
10 ounces fresh or frozen green peas

Place the veal cubes in a large bowl and sprinkle with the salt and pepper, making sure the meat is coated on all sides. Add the flour and mix until well coated.

Heat the oil in a large nonstick sauté pan on medium heat for 2 minutes. Add the meat and brown well on all sides, about 3 minutes. Transfer the cooked veal to a bowl and set aside.

Pour the oil reserved from the sauté pan (there should be 2½ tablespoons – if not, add additional oil to make that amount) into a medium pot or Dutch oven set on medium-low heat. Cook the finely chopped carrot, onion, garlic, celery, rosemary, basil and bay leaves for 5 minutes. Add the browned veal and the juices that have accumulated in the bowl, increase the heat to medium-high and cook for 1 minute. Add the wine and cook until reduced by half, about 4 minutes.

Sometimes the winters were so frigid in the Veneto region where my grandmother lived, that my mother would insist that Nonna Adele come down and spend the harshest months in Sicily, where the weather was much milder.

Even though she had the look of an old, mild-mannered lady, Nonna Adele was a firecracker. While I know she was always happy to spend time with her "due diavoletti" (two little devils), Mario and me, she felt at loose ends in our apartment. After all, she came from a farm where there was always some kind of chore to be done. So, with everyone's blessing she made our kitchen her domain. I immediately volunteered to be her kitchen assistant.

The recipe that follows is the first meal I cooked on my own, at the tender age of 10, under Nonna Adele's supervision. Every time I prepare it I can feel her smiling next to me, gently guiding my young hands with her's.

"Ciao, Nonna!"

CONTINUED ON FOLLOWING PAGE

Meanwhile, drain the tomatoes and chop them, reserving the juices separately. Add the chicken stock and the reserved tomato juices to the pot, bring to a boil, and cook for 3 minutes. Stir in the chopped tomatoes and bring back to a boil. Place a cover on the pot, leaving it just slightly ajar, reduce the heat and simmer for 30 minutes, stirring often to prevent sticking or burning. Stir in the potatoes, cover and simmer for 30 minutes, stirring often. Stir in the cubed carrots, cover and simmer for 30 minutes, stirring often. Stir in the peas, and simmer uncovered for 30 minutes, stirring often.

COOK'S TIP

You can regulate the thickness of the stew by simmering with or without the cover on the pot: without the cover, you will have a much thicker stew.

CARNE ALLA PIZZAIOLA

VEAL CUTLETS PIZZA STYLE

Serves 4

INGREDIENTS

1 (28-ounce) can peeled Italian tomatoes
4 teaspoons olive oil
4 garlic cloves, sliced
¼ teaspoon red pepper flakes
10 fresh basil leaves
¼ teaspoon oregano
½ chicken bouillon cube, crumbled
1½ pounds veal slices, pounded thin
¼ teaspoon salt
¼ teaspoon black pepper

Pour the tomatoes into a bowl and break them up into small pieces.
Pour the olive oil into a large sauté pan on medium-high heat and cook the garlic and red pepper flakes until the garlic just starts to brown, about 3 minutes. Add the broken tomatoes with their juices, the basil, oregano, and bouillon cube and cook for 10 minutes. Sprinkle the meat with the salt and pepper, add to the sauce and cook for 5 minutes. Be careful not to overcook the meat; watch carefully for the color change to indicate the meat is ready.

I'd like to present you with a little culinary treasure that has graced some of the best dinner menus at the Stellino household. This simple recipe overflows with a character all its own. You can easily build on it to create your own personal variation. Serve it with a steaming side of my Garlic Mashed Potatoes (see page 112) and if you're like me, pour the gravy on top.

When my mother, Massimiliana, made this dish we'd always have this little game of words. "Mamma, la pizza c'é?" (Mamma, is the pizza there?) "Si, che c'é!" (Yes, it is here!) "Dov'é?" (Where?) "In padella con la carne." (It is in the pan with the meat.) As you can see, it is not exactly a sample of deep, meaningful dialogue, but to me it was fun.

Even now that I'm supposedly a mature man of the world, I still play this game with my mom. Time has been gracious to her. Her features have grown old without shadowing her natural beauty and when we play like this I'm still her little "Nicolino" and she'll always be my Mamma.

I was first introduced to this dish when I was 17 years old and my father took me to the gallery opening of Renato Guttuso, an important Sicilian painter. It was a very important affair held in an old and

prestigious building. Needless to say, I was in awe of what I saw. As a teenager, basketball and girls were the extent of my daily interests. This event, however, got my attention, for it was like a page out of the society section. The foods served were all new and exciting, but the shrimp wrapped in prosciutto was my absolute favorite.

Lentils are not a common accompaniment for shrimp, but please take my word for it, you'll be amazed by this incredible combination. My friend, chef Celestino Drago, introduced me to this combination.

Serves 4

INGREDIENTS

½ pound Italian-style prosciutto, sliced paper thin
20 raw shrimp, 16-20 count, shelled and deveined with tail left on
2 tablespoons olive oil
1 recipe Lentils with Tomatoes and Onions (see page 105)

Wrap one slice of prosciutto around each shrimp, making sure the body is completely covered, while leaving the tail and the last piece of shell exposed. Squeeze it tightly in your palm to make sure the prosciutto clings to the shrimp.

Coat a large nonstick sauté pan with the olive oil and cook on high heat for 2 minutes. Add the shrimp and cook 2 minutes on each side. The shrimp are cooked when the prosciutto is well browned and like a second skin and the tail and the shell have turned pink.

To serve, cover the bottom of each plate with a layer of warm lentils and top with five cooked shrimp.

GAMBERI AL COCCIO

SHRIMP IN THE POT

Serves 4

INGREDIENTS

4 tablespoons olive oil

4 garlic cloves, thinly sliced

2 teaspoons anchovy paste

2 pounds raw shrimp, in their shells (11–12 count)

¼ teaspoon red pepper flakes

¼ teaspoon oregano

½ teaspoon salt

¼ teaspoon black pepper

1 cup wine

1 cup clam juice or Shrimp Stock (see page 141)

½ cup Tomato Sauce (see page 137)

3 teaspoons chopped fresh parsley

4 large slices Italian bread, toasted and rubbed with garlic

In a Dutch oven or a large saucepan with a heavy bottom, cook the olive oil, garlic and anchovy paste on medium-high heat until the garlic starts to sizzle, about 2-3 minutes. Add the shrimp, red pepper flakes, oregano, salt and pepper, tossing until the shrimp are well coated, and cook for 2 minutes. Add the wine, clam juice or shrimp stock, tomato sauce and parsley and bring to a boil. Remove the shrimp and set aside. Continue cooking the broth over high heat for 3 minutes.

Reduce the heat to a simmer, return the partially cooked shrimp to the pan and simmer for 2 minutes. Turn off the heat.

Place the toasted bread in the middle of a pasta bowl. Top with the cooked shrimp and ladle with all the sauce. Let it marinate for a minute. Add another bowl in the middle of the table to accommodate the discarded shrimp shells and the dish is now ready to be served.

COOK'S TIP

The best shrimp to use for this recipe are the 11–12 count, pink-shelled Gulf of Mexico shrimp. They are big enough to take the cooking time with a good margin of error and they taste delicious. I'd suggest not using anything smaller than 20–25 count, because they will become tough before they have time to flavor the sauce.

The name of this recipe comes from the glazed terra-cotta pot that was traditionally used in its preparation. The simple ingredients are part of that inexpensive everyday fare so common to the fisherman's diet. The shrimp, which in today's supermarkets often reach filet mignon prices, were in the old days nothing more than part of the daily catch.

During my college days, I often prepared this dish for my friends. I'd like to think it was my charming personality that accounted for the popularity of my dinner parties during those low budget school days, but I suspect that this traditional workingman's dish, coupled with the ravenous appetites of my old college buddies, deserves most of the credit.

While it may seem unusual to cook the shrimp in their shell, in this particular case the shells impart the characteristic flavor base and guarantees that the shrimp will be tender and juicy. In fact, if you have an adventurous spirit, I think the flavor of the sauce increases significantly if you use shrimp with the head intact.

My father gloried in his reputation as a locally renowned fish chef. Fishermen would save the best of their catch for him, as long as he would bring them a taste of his special dishes.

As a young child I wasn't very excited about fish, but the following recipe was always a favorite of mine because of its sweet-sour tomato sauce. A significant credit for the popularity of this dish should also go to my mother. Knowing how much I disliked fish, she called it "Bistecca di Mare al Sugo" (Ocean Steak in Tomato Sauce.) That name really caught my imagination and ultimately conquered my palate.

Serves 4

INGREDIENTS

3 tablespoons olive oil
2 tablespoons chopped shallots
4 garlic cloves, thinly sliced
¼ cup white or red wine
1 cup clam juice
1 cup Tomato Sauce (see page 137)
2 tablespoons drained capers
½ cup halved and pitted black olives, preferably Kalamata
or Italian-style oil-cured varieties
3 tablespoons chopped fresh Italian parsley
¼ teaspoon red pepper flakes (optional)
1 tablespoon lemon juice (optional)
1½ teaspoons balsamic vinegar
2¼ teaspoons sugar
4 (6-ounce) tuna steaks, about ¾ inch thick
¼ teaspoon salt
¼ teaspoon black pepper

To prepare the sauce, pour 2 tablespoons of the olive oil into a large sauté pan and cook the shallots and garlic over medium-high heat until the garlic starts to sizzle, 2 minutes. Add the wine, being careful to avoid splatters, and deglaze the pan, shaking gently, for 1 minute.

Add the clam juice, tomato sauce, capers, olives and parsley. For a spicy sauce, add the red pepper flakes. If you prefer a tart finish, add the lemon juice. Bring to a boil, stir in the vinegar and sugar, reduce the heat and simmer for 10 minutes, stirring occasionally with a wooden spoon while you prepare the fish.

Sprinkle both sides of the tuna with the salt and pepper. Pour the remaining olive oil into a nonstick pan large enough to fit the steaks and heat on high until the oil is almost smoking. Add the tuna and cook for 1 minute on each side. The edges should be nicely browned while the fish is still raw inside. Remove from the heat and transfer the tuna to the simmering sauce, cover and simmer 2 minutes. Turn over, cover and simmer 3 more minutes for medium-well done steaks.

COOK'S TIP

This recipe will also work well with swordfish. The amount of vinegar and sugar in this recipe is for a medium sweet-and-sour finish. Increase or decrease the ingredients according to your taste.

GROUPER CUTLET WITH BREAD FRITTERS

My father considered the grouper the king of all fish. While I might not share his enthusiasm on this particular matter, I will admit that his preparation of this fish was truly fit for a king. By using Italian-style bread crumbs for the fillets, you'll greatly enhance grouper's naturally delicate flavor.

But please, do not limit yourself to grouper. Any firm-fleshed fish, such as halibut or monkfish, will work. I encourage you to experiment – you'll be pleasantly surprised by the versatility of this recipe.

Serves 4

INGREDIENTS

4 (4-ounce) grouper fillets, about ½ inch thick
1 cup white wine
2 tablespoons lemon juice
3 garlic cloves, finely chopped
1½ tablespoons chopped fresh parsley
¼ teaspoon salt
⅛ teaspoon black pepper
3 eggs
2½ cups Italian Bread Crumbs (see page 142)
¼ cup olive oil
1 whole lemon, quartered

Wash and dry the grouper fillets, removing any remaining bones. Place the fillets in a deep casserole and set aside.

In a medium bowl, mix the wine, lemon juice, garlic, parsley, salt and pepper and whisk well. Pour over the fish and refrigerate for 30 minutes, turning the fish once after 15 minutes.

Place the eggs in a large bowl and beat lightly. Spread the bread crumbs out on a large plate. Dip the marinated grouper fillets in the eggs, then dredge them in the bread crumbs, making sure they're completely coated, and set aside. Reserve the leftover marinade, eggs and bread crumbs for Bread Fritters (see the Cook's Tip).

Pour the oil into a large sauté pan on high heat and cook until hot. Reduce the heat to medium, add the fish fillets and cook until well browned, about 3-5 minutes. Turn over and cook for 3-5 minutes. Transfer the cooked fish to thickly layered paper towels and with another paper towel, gently press on top to absorb any excess oil. Serve with a lemon quarter on top of each fillet and Bread Fritters on the side (see the Cook's Tip).

COOK'S TIP

Use the leftover eggs, bread crumbs and marinade to make great bread fritters. Mix the leftover bread crumbs with the leftover eggs and ¼ cup of the reserved marinade or an equal amount of milk, stirring until you have a smooth batter. Pour the batter into the same sauté pan in which you sautéed the fish, and cook for 3 minutes. Transfer the pancake to a paper towel and pat off the excess oil with another paper towel. Cut into four equal slices and serve. You could also shape the batter into little pancakes – it's your choice.

E*veryone in my family was an outspoken food critic. My father, especially, was a tyrant, feared and despised by all chefs within a five mile radius. I know this may seem a bit exaggerated, but allow me to put my words in proper perspective. My father was unable to lie gracefully, was not kind in his criticism and to make it worse, most of the time he was right. His favorite reproach for a badly cooked fish dish was, "This fish died twice, once when it was fished out of the ocean, the second time when you cooked it." Given this bit of background, it is not hard to imagine why my mother was not eager to eat out. The few times we did eat out were during our travels or for some special occasion.*

It was during one of these family trips around Sicily that we ended up in a little restaurant close to the city of Messina. It was one o'clock in the afternoon and we had not eaten since breakfast.

Serves 4 to 6

INGREDIENTS

4 tablespoons water
1 onion, finely chopped
5 tablespoons olive oil
3 tablespoons finely chopped garlic
6 tablespoons raisins, plumped in hot water for 20 minutes and drained
6 tablespoons pine nuts
¼ teaspoon red pepper flakes
½ teaspoon finely chopped lemon zest
4 tablespoons Marsala wine
2 pounds loin-cut swordfish, cut into ¼-inch slices, skin removed
2 egg yolks
1 tablespoon fresh lemon juice
4 tablespoons grated Romano cheese
2 ¼ cups Italian Bread Crumbs (see page 142)
2 cups Tomato Sauce (see page 137)
1 cup clam juice or Shrimp Stock (see page 141)
4 tablespoons finely chopped fresh parsley

Pour the water into a nonstick sauté pan, add the chopped onion and cook over high heat until the water evaporates. Add 2 tablespoons of the olive oil, 1 tablespoon of the garlic, the raisins, pine nuts, red pepper flakes and lemon zest. Continue cooking, stirring continuously, over medium heat for 3 minutes. Deglaze the pan with the Marsala wine and transfer its contents to a bowl.

Pound the swordfish slices between two pieces of plastic wrap, being careful not to rip the flesh. Once pounded, cut them into sixteen 3 x 4-inch rectangles. Finely chop all the left over pieces and set aside.

Add the chopped swordfish, egg yolks, lemon juice, Romano cheese, the remaining garlic, and 2 cups of the bread crumbs to the bowl with the onion mixture. Mix well to incorporate all the ingredients.

Lay the swordfish rectangles on a chopping board or a kitchen table. Place equal amounts of the filling on each slice of fish, fold the edges inward and form about 16 rolls. The stuffing will be pretty sticky and if you press well with your fingers, the rolls will keep their shape without the need of toothpicks. Coat the rolls with the remaining bread crumbs.

Pour the remaining oil into a large nonstick sauté pan and warm over high heat until almost smoking. Sauté the rolls, seam-side-down, until golden brown, 2 minutes on each side, and remove to a serving dish. Pour out any remaining oil in the pan and wipe the pan clean. Add the tomato sauce, clam juice or shrimp stock and fresh parsley to the pan and bring to a boil over medium heat. Add the fish rolls and simmer, basting with the sauce, for 8-10 minutes over low heat until well cooked.

COOK'S TIPS

For a variation on this recipe, add a vinegar/sugar reduction of 3 table-spoons vinegar and 2 tablespoons sugar reduced by half over high heat, to the sauce before simmering the fish rolls.

For a very sophisticated presentation, add 1 teaspoon cocoa powder and 1½ tablespoons cubed, parboiled celery to the sauce.

The owner chef came out to greet us and to tell us about his specialties. My father, as always, threw down a challenge: "Please bring us what you do best." My mother's eyes rolled back in disbelief while my brother and I elbowed each other in anticipation of the upcoming disaster. The food was brought to the table and we attacked it like hungry wolves. The more we ate the better it tasted. Even my father was eating and smiling. My mother was enjoying the silence, feeling the stress of the situation slowly dissipating.

The owner/chef came by a little while later to check on us, asking the loaded question, "Was everything okay?" Everyone froze – our eyes fixed on my father. He lifted his head slowly, cleared his throat with a light cough, and began to speak. "This fish died once when it was taken out of the sea. You gave it a new life when you prepared it for us."

That was the first time I had Involtini di Pesce Spada.

Pitello was a young fishmonger who had a shop in Il Capo, one of the famous traditional open air markets of Palermo.

Pitello had barely finished elementary school when he had to

abandon his studies to help out in the family business. He made up for his lack of formal education with a naturally engaging personality and a philosophical sense of humor with strong satirical overtones.

Pitello always brought fish for my friends and me to cook and we provided the wine and dessert. He was a gifted cook and introduced this dish at one of our lunches.

"Sfincione" means it is in the style of Sicilian pizza: cooked in a deep dish with the traditional toppings of tomato sauce, onions, oregano, cheese and bread crumbs.

Serves 4

INGREDIENTS

2 onions, thinly sliced
1 tablespoon lemon juice
¼ teaspoon oregano
¼ teaspoon red pepper flakes
2 teaspoons chopped garlic
¾ cup water
2 teaspoons chopped fresh parsley
¾ cup Tomato Sauce (see page 137)
¼ cup Chicken Stock (see page 139)
1 cup clam juice
2 teaspoons sugar
4 (6-8 ounce) swordfish fillets, about ½ inch thick, skin removed
2 tablespoons olive oil
¼ teaspoon salt
¼ teaspoon black pepper
⅓ cup + 4 tablespoons Italian Bread Crumbs (see page 142)
4 tablespoons grated Romano cheese

Preheat the oven to 450° F.

Place the sliced onions, lemon juice, oregano, red pepper flakes and chopped garlic in a medium nonstick saucepan and cover with the water. Bring to a boil and simmer until all the water has evaporated, 10-12 minutes. Add the parsley, tomato sauce, chicken stock, clam juice and sugar, bring to a boil and simmer 8-10 minutes, until the sauce is very thick.

Pound the fish slices to flatten them slightly. Brush them with 1 tablespoon of the olive oil and sprinkle with the salt and pepper. Coat with ⅓ cup of the bread crumbs, pressing well to make a uniform coating.

Pour the remaining tablespoon of olive oil into a large ovenproof dish, making sure the bottom is completely covered. Place the swordfish slices in the dish, top with the sauce, and sprinkle with the Romano cheese and the remaining bread crumbs. Put in the preheated oven, reduce the heat to 400° F and cook for 10-15 minutes, testing for doneness after 10 minutes.

FRITTATA DI PASTA

PASTA FRITTATA

Serves 4 to 6

INGREDIENTS

8 ounces long pasta – linguine, spaghetti, spaghettini or bucatini
2½ tablespoons chopped fresh basil
2½ tablespoons chopped fresh parsley
1½ tablespoons chopped garlic
5 tablespoons grated Romano cheese
3 tablespoons grated Parmigiano Reggiano cheese
1½ teaspoons salt
⅛ teaspoon pepper
8 eggs
3 tablespoons olive oil

Preheat the oven to 350° F.

Cook the pasta in a large pot of boiling water according to package directions for just tender. Drain well, cut it into 2-inch pieces and transfer to a large bowl. Add the basil, parsley, garlic, Romano cheese, Parmigiano Reggiano cheese, ½ teaspoon of the salt and the pepper and mix well.

In another bowl, beat the eggs and the remaining 1 teaspoon of the salt with a wire whisk. Add the eggs to the cooked pasta mixture and mix well.

Heat the olive oil in an ovenproof 12-inch nonstick skillet on high heat until sizzling, about 2 minutes. Pour in the egg and pasta mixture and cook for 2 minutes. Place in the preheated oven and cook for 15 minutes. Turn the frittata over and cook for another 15 minutes. Slide the frittata out onto a serving dish. It can be eaten warm or at room temperature.

COOK'S TIP

It might be easier for you to turn the frittata on a flat pan cover or dinner plate and then slide it back into the pan. To do this, slide the frittata out of the pan onto the flat dish, put the pan over the frittata on the dish and turn the dish and pan over at the same time so that the fritttata is now cooked-side-up in the pan.

Springtime in Sicily: Wild flowers start to cover the gently rolling hills of the countryside around Palermo, and the Stellinos and their clan of friends are already on the lookout for an outdoor dining adventure. For our most satisfying picnics, frittatas were always on the menu. This recipe is one of the best uses I know for leftover pasta.

FRITTATA DI PATATE

POTATO FRITTATA

Serves 4 to 6

INGREDIENTS

4 new potatoes, peeled and diced into ½-inch cubes
6 tablespoons olive oil
2½ tablespoons chopped fresh rosemary
1½ teaspoons chopped garlic
¼ teaspoon pepper
8 eggs
1¼ teaspoons salt

My mother had an important weapon to use against my father's blatant disregard for preplanning: the Massimiliana One-Eyed Stare. I think it must be one of the most admonishing facial expressions on record, sending shivers of fear down the spine of the recipient. Mamma's right brow would arch upward above her steely blue eye while the left brow would frown downward, leaving only a menacing slit .

But once she had reduced my father to shivering jelly, Mamma would cheerfully take on the challenge of an impromptu dinner entree and come up with a wonderful recipe, such as this frittata.

Place the potatoes in a medium saucepan, cover with water, bring to a boil and boil until just tender, about 20 minutes. Drain well.

Preheat the oven to 375° F.

Cook 3 tablespoons of the oil in a 12-inch nonstick skillet set on high heat until it sizzles, about 2 minutes. Add the cooked potatoes and cook for 5 minutes, stirring once. Add 2 tablespoons of the rosemary, reduce the heat to medium-high and cook for 5 minutes, stirring once. Add 1 teaspoon of the chopped garlic and ⅛ teaspoon of the pepper and cook for 5 minutes, stirring once. Transfer to a large bowl and set aside.

In a large bowl, beat the eggs, ¼ teaspoon of the salt and the remaining rosemary with a whisk and set aside. Stir in the potatoes and mix well.

Cook the remaining 3 tablespoons of oil in a nonstick ovenproof skillet until sizzling, about 2 minutes. Add the potato-egg mixture and cook for 2 minutes, stirring to prevent sticking. Place the skillet in the preheated oven and cook for 15 minutes. Turn the frittata over and cook for another 15 minutes. Slide it out onto a serving dish, sprinkle with the remaining salt and eat warm or at room temperature. The flavors ripen beautifully if held overnight in the refrigerator.

COOK'S TIP

If you do not have a 12-inch sauté pan, you can use two 8-inch pans.

FRITTATA DI CIPOLLE

ONION FRITTATA

Serves 4 to 6

INGREDIENTS

6 tablespoons olive oil
4 onions, peeled and sliced
¼ teaspoon red pepper flakes
1½ teaspoons dried thyme
1 teaspoon salt
⅛ teaspoon black pepper
1½ teaspoons chopped garlic
5 eggs

Cook 3 tablespoons of the oil in a 12-inch nonstick skillet set on high heat until it sizzles, about 2 minutes. Add the onions, red pepper flakes and thyme. Mix well, reduce the heat to medium-low and cook for 30 minutes, stirring every 5 minutes to prevent sticking.

Add ½ teaspoon of the salt, the pepper and 1 teaspoon of the garlic, reduce the heat to low and cook for 30 minutes, stirring every 10 minutes. Transfer the onion mixture to a large bowl.

In another bowl, beat the eggs, the remaining salt and the remaining ½ teaspoon of the chopped garlic with a wire whisk. Add this mixture to the onions and mix well.

Preheat the oven to 350° F.

Cook the remaining 3 tablespoons of the olive oil in a 10-inch nonstick ovenproof skillet set on high heat until it sizzles, about 2 minutes. Pour in the onion and egg mixture and cook for 2 minutes. Place the skillet in the preheated oven and cook for 12 minutes. Turn the frittata over and cook 12 minutes more. Slide the frittata out onto a serving dish. It can be eaten warm, but it tastes better refrigerated overnight and eaten at room temperature the next day.

COOK'S TIP

The correct cooking of the onions depends on proper temperature control. To prevent burning or sticking, monitor the onions carefully during the last 30 minutes of cooking, reducing the heat if they start to stick or burn.

The frittata makes a most effective, last-minute entree for brunch, a casual dinner or a picnic. Once you master the basic technique, a whole world of mix-and-match combinations will open in front of your eyes. The art of the frittata is the Italian version of culinary recycling: it's most creative applied to leftover meat, cheese and vegetables lying abandoned on your refrigerator shelf. The secret to the success in this version lies in cooking the onions to a deep golden brown, which makes them extra-sweet.

Well what are you waiting for? Crack those eggs and let's get to work!

Frittatas can be made with whatever ingredients are on hand in your refrigerator. I encourage you to try variations using this recipe as a base. For instance, I look in my refrigerator now and find 2 tablespoons of chopped sun-dried tomatoes and 1 cup of crumbled Gorgonzola cheese. The possibilities are literally endless.

Serves 4 to 6

INGREDIENTS
6 tablespoons olive oil
4 onions, sliced
¼ teaspoon red pepper flakes
1½ teaspoons dried thyme
1 teaspoon salt
⅛ teaspoon black pepper
2 teaspoons chopped garlic
1 pound sweet Italian sausage, removed from the casing
2 tablespoons chopped fresh parsley
8 eggs

Cook 3 tablespoons of the oil in a 12-inch nonstick skillet set on high heat until sizzling, about 2 minutes. Add the onions, red pepper flakes and thyme, mix well, reduce the heat to medium-low and cook for 30 minutes, stirring every 5 minutes to prevent sticking.

Add ½ teaspoon of the salt, the pepper, and 1 teaspoon of the garlic, reduce the heat to low and cook for 30 minutes, stirring every 10 minutes. Transfer the onion mixture to a large bowl.

Preheat the oven to 350° F.

In another nonstick skillet, brown the sausage and discard the rendered fat. Add the browned sausage and the parsley to the cooked onions and mix well.

In a large bowl, beat the eggs with the remaining salt and the remaining garlic. Stir into the onion/sausage mixture.

Cook the remaining 3 tablespoons of the oil in a 12-inch nonstick oven-proof skillet on medium-high heat until sizzling, about 2 minutes. Pour in the frittata mixture and cook for 2 minutes, stirring once. Bake in the preheated oven for 15 minutes. Turn the frittata over and bake for 15 minutes more.

It tastes great warm, but the tastes mature beautifully if the frittatta is refrigerated overnight, then brought back to room temperature to serve the next day.

CONTORNI

Side Dishes

B R A I S E D   B R O C C O L I

Serves 4 to 6

INGREDIENTS
4 tablespoons olive oil
5 garlic cloves, sliced
¼ teaspoon red pepper flakes
2 pounds broccoli, cut into 1-inch pieces, stems included,
parboiled for 3 minutes
½ cup of the broccoli cooking water
½ chicken bouillon cube, crumbled
salt to taste

Pour the oil into a large sauté pan set on medium heat and cook the garlic and red pepper flakes for 2 minutes. Add the parboiled broccoli pieces, toss until well coated with the oil, and cook for 2 minutes. Add ½ cup of the reserved cooking water and the bouillon cube and bring to a boil. Reduce the heat and simmer, with the cover just slightly ajar, for 10 minutes. Taste for salt.

This dish is good enough to make anyone believe in magic. Just throw a few simple ingredients into a pan, cover and cook for a while over low heat, and – presto – a spectacular result in flavor and presentation.

Add a touch of cream, a bit of chicken stock and a couple of pulses in the food processor and you have a fabulous pasta sauce.

The following recipe showcases the versatility of this fantastic vegetable, often called poor man's caviar, which is so richly portrayed in the Sicilian culinary tradition. I was originally exposed to this dish while in Agrigento with my family during a weekend outing.

Agrigento is a town in Sicily renowned for "La Valle Dei Templi," (The Valley of Temples,) which is a magnificent archeological site that covers the whole valley surrounding the city. The gently sloping terrain, filled with a multitude of Grecian temples dating back to the Greek colonization of Sicily in the fourth century B.C., is a truly impressive sight.

During our visits to this area, we would have lunch at a local trattoria. The following recipe, one of our favorites, was gently but stubbornly pried from the pursed lips of the chef/operator, a rough-looking character who, as many before him, fell prey to my mother's irresistible charm.

EGGPLANT FRITTERS

Serves 6 to 8

INGREDIENTS

3 eggplants, about 1½ pounds each
½ teaspoon salt
6 tablespoons olive oil
2 cups Italian Bread Crumbs (see page 142)
3 eggs
1 cup grated Romano cheese
1½ tablespoons chopped fresh mint

AGRIGENTO SAUCE:

2 cups Tomato Sauce (see page 137)
1 cup drained eggplant juice
2 teaspoons sugar
2½ tablespoons finely chopped fresh mint

Preheat the oven to 425° F.

Cut the stem end off each eggplant, then cut them in half lengthwise. Score the cut side of each half, being careful not to cut the skin. Thoroughly rub the salt over the cut sides of each eggplant half. Set the eggplant halves aside on paper towels, cut-side-down, and let them drain for about 20 minutes.

Line two baking sheets with parchment paper. Dry the eggplant halves and use 2 tablespoons of the olive oil to brush the tops and bottoms of the eggplants as well as the parchment paper on the baking sheets. Place the eggplants, cut-side-down, on the parchment paper and bake for 45-55 minutes, until they are completely cooked and dent easily when you poke the skin. Remove from the oven and let cool. Scoop out the roasted flesh and transfer to a colander with a bowl underneath. Let drain for 40 minutes, stirring once. Reserve 1 cup of the drained eggplant juices for the sauce.

Transfer the drained eggplant flesh to a large bowl and stir in the bread crumbs, eggs, cheese and mint. Mix well, cover and refrigerate overnight to let the flavors mature.

To prepare the fritters, shape the eggplant mixture into balls 1½ inches in diameter. You should have approximately 35-40. Pour 2 tablespoons of the oil into a large, nonstick sauté pan on high heat, add half the balls and brown on all sides, about 5 minutes. Wipe the pan clean, pour in the remaining 2 tablespoons of oil and repeat the process.

Place the warm eggplant fritters in a serving bowl and top with 2 cups of the sauce.

AGRIGENTO SAUCE:

Liquefy the tomato sauce and eggplant juice in a food processor for 2 minutes. Strain the mixture through a wire mesh strainer into a saucepan. Bring the sauce to a simmer over medium heat, add the sugar and mint, stir well and simmer for 10 minutes.

COOK'S TIP

Frying the eggplant balls requires some technique, especially in turning. An excellent tool is a large wooden spoon. Using the edge of the pan as a support, turn the balls over by pushing upward and over with the concave part of the spoon. Remember, move gently, the fritters are very soft and they will break if you're too forceful.

My mother developed quite an expertise in the Sicilian culinary arts. This feat is even more impressive when you take into account the fact that she was not Sicilian and not really trained in the art of cooking.

She developed her passion to great heights, and what follows is one of her most impressive recipes. It was liberally adapted from a rather pompous book about the cuisine of the Sicilian nobility, which had better photographs than recipes, but which Mother found a great source of inspiration. If you compare this recipe to Eggplant Fritters (see pages 100-101) you'll be amazed at how similar preparations yield such different results. In its finished form, this dish is quite a spectacular sight and yet surprisingly simple to prepare.

SFORNATO DI MELANZANE

TERRINE OF ROASTED EGGPLANT

Serves 6 to 8

INGREDIENTS
4 eggplants, about 1½ pounds each
¾ tablespoon salt
4 tablespoons olive oil
4 eggs
1 cup grated Romano cheese
1¼ cups Italian Bread Crumbs (see page 142)
2¼ teaspoons butter
¼ pound goat cheese, cubed

ROASTED EGGPLANT SAUCE:
2 cups Tomato Sauce (see page 137)
1 cup reserved roasted eggplant juice
2 teaspoons sugar
2 tablespoons chopped fresh basil
1 tablespoon olive oil
6 tablespoons finely diced celery

Preheat the oven to 425° F.

Cut the stem ends off all the eggplants. Cut 3 eggplants in half lengthwise and score the flesh with a sharp knife, making sure you don't cut through the skin. Rub the cut surface of the eggplants well with ½ tablespoon of the salt. Set the eggplant halves aside on paper towels, cut-side-down, and let them drain for 20 minutes.

Cut the fourth eggplant in half lengthwise and cut into ¼-inch slices also lengthwise. Sprinkle with the remaining salt. Lay the slices on top of one another in a colander. Place a dish on top and weight it with about 1½ pounds (a can of tomatoes will do). Drain for 20 minutes.

Line the bottoms of two 18 x 13-inch baking sheets with parchment paper. Dry the cut surfaces of the eggplant halves and brush the parchment and eggplant with 3 tablespoons of the oil. Place them on the baking sheets, cut-side-down, and bake in the preheated oven 45-55 minutes. The eggplants are completely cooked when they dent easily as you poke the skin. Do not cook them more than 1 hour as they burn easily once they are cooked. Remove them from the oven and let cool for a few minutes.

Meanwhile, dry the eggplant slices with a paper towel. Line another sheet pan with parchment paper. Brush the paper and the eggplant with the remaining olive oil and cook for 25-35 minutes, until golden brown. Set aside.

Using a large spoon, scoop the cooked flesh out of the roasted eggplant halves. Discard the skin and place the flesh in a colander with a bowl underneath to catch the juices. Drain for 40 minutes, stirring once. Save 1 cup of the juices that have drained from the eggplant to use in the sauce. Discard the rest or save it for other uses.

NOW WE'RE READY TO ASSEMBLE OUR SFORNATO!

Preheat the oven to 400° F.

Separate the 4 eggs. Mix the yolks, Romano cheese and 1 cup of the bread crumbs with the roasted eggplant flesh. Beat the egg whites until they form stiff peaks, then fold them gently into the eggplant mixture.

Rub the inside of a standard glass loaf pan (8½ x 4½ x 2½ inches) with 1 tablespoon of the butter and coat with the remaining bread crumbs. Line the bottom of the loaf pan with the 2 largest slices of eggplant; place the remaining slices around the edges, standing up and overlapping slightly. They should extend above the rim by about ⅓ of their length so that you can fold them over the roasted filling.

Put half the eggplant mixture into the pan as the first layer and top it with the goat cheese as the middle layer. Cover with the remaining eggplant mixture and fold over the overlapping eggplant slices. Bake in the preheated oven for 45 minutes.

This dish can be served right away by inverting it on a serving tray and cutting it at the table, but I strongly recommend that you let it rest at least overnight in the refrigerator. When ready to serve, invert it onto a cutting board, cut into serving slices and reheat in a preheated 350° F oven on a parchment-lined sheet pan for 25 minutes. It can be prepared up to 4 days in advance.

CONTINUED ON FOLLOWING PAGE

ROASTED EGGPLANT SAUCE:

Liquefy the tomato sauce and eggplant juice in a food processor for about 2 minutes. Strain through a wire mesh strainer into a saucepan. Add the sugar and basil and bring to a simmer over medium heat. Reduce the heat to medium-low and cook for 10 minutes, stirring twice.

Heat the olive oil in a nonstick pan set on over high heat until sizzling. Add the celery and sauté until brown. Drain well and add to the simmering sauce until it is finished cooking. The sauce is now complete. It can be made up to 4 days in advance and kept in the refrigerator. Heat through before serving.

Pour a pool of the hot sauce on each dinner plate and place a slice of the eggplant terrine on top.

LENTICCHIE ALL'ANTICA CON POMODORO E CIPOLLE

LENTILS WITH TOMATOES AND ONIONS

Serves 4 to 5

INGREDIENTS

3 tablespoons olive oil
½ onion, chopped
3 garlic cloves, chopped
⅛ teaspoon red pepper flakes
1 (1-pound) can peeled Italian tomatoes
1 tablespoon chopped fresh parsley
1 tablespoon chopped fresh basil
1 cup dried lentils
2 cups Chicken Stock (see page 139)
¾ teaspoon salt

The surprisingly commanding flavor of this lentil recipe could elevate it from a fantastic side dish to an entree on its own. I especially like it with my favorite, Shrimp Wrapped in Prosciutto (see page 84).

Heat the olive oil in a medium saucepan set on high heat for 1 minute. Reduce the heat to low, add the onion, garlic and red pepper flakes, and cook 1 minute.

Meanwhile, drain the tomatoes, reserving the juices separately. Chop the tomatoes and add them to the pan along with the parsley and basil and cook for 3 minutes. Add the lentils, stir well and cook for 2 minutes. Pour in the stock, the reserved tomato juices and the salt and bring to a boil. Reduce the heat to a simmer, cover and cook for 25 minutes. Transfer 1½ cups of the lentil mixture to a blender and process to a creamy consistency. Stir it back into the saucepan, cover and simmer for 10 minutes. The lentils are ready when they are tender to the bite.

COOK'S TIP

Different types of lentils have different cooking times and different liquid absorption rates. Be your own judge as to whether to add more liquid to obtain the consistency you like best.

This dish is often referred to as "Caviale del bosco" (caviar from the woods). The taste of this recipe will change depending on what combination of wild mushrooms you're able to find. Porcini, fresh or dried, will always provide you with excellent results.

Serves 4

INGREDIENTS
4 tablespoons olive oil
1½ pounds diced mushrooms, at least 3 different varieties
¼ + ⅛ teaspoon salt
⅛ teaspoon black pepper
⅛ teaspoon red pepper flakes
4 garlic cloves, chopped
1½ tablespoons chopped fresh parsley
¼ cup white wine
¼ cup dry Marsala or Port wine
¼ cup heavy cream

In a large, nonstick sauté pan, cook the olive oil over high heat until it is very hot, almost smoking, about 3 minutes. Add the diced mushrooms and cook for 2 minutes without stirring. Stir and cook 1 more minute.

Add the ¼ teaspoon salt, the black pepper, red pepper flakes, garlic and parsley. Cook 2 minutes, stirring continously. Add the white wine, Marsala and mushroom liquid if you used dried mushrooms. Cook until almost evaporated, about 3 minutes. Add the cream and the additional ⅛ teaspoon of salt if needed. Cook, stirring occasionally, until the mushrooms are well coated, about 2 more minutes. Enjoy!

COOK'S TIPS
Do not use dried porcini mushrooms exclusively for this dish. Always mix them with other fresh mushroom varieties in these proportions: ½ ounce dried to 1¼ pounds fresh.

If you are using dried porcini mushrooms, soak them in ¾ cup hot chicken stock until soft, about 30 minutes. Drain, reserving the mushrooms and soaking water separately.

CIPOLLINE IN AGRO DOLCE

SWEET AND SOUR PEARL ONIONS

Serves 4

INGREDIENTS

2 (10-ounce) packages frozen petite pearl onions
1 tablespoon olive oil
2 garlic cloves, chopped
2 tablespoons chopped fresh parsley stems
⅛ teaspoon red pepper flakes
½ cup Chicken Stock (see page 139)
1 tablespoon chopped fresh parsley leaves
6 tablespoons balsamic vinegar
3 tablespoons sugar
2 tablespoons butter

Parboil the frozen onions for about 2-3 minutes. Drain well and set aside.
Pour the oil into a medium sauté pan set on medium-high heat and cook
the garlic, parsley stems, and red pepper flakes for 5 minutes. Add the onions,
chicken stock and parsley, stir well and bring to a boil. Reduce the heat and
simmer 10 minutes.

In a small nonstick sauté pan, cook the vinegar and sugar over medium
heat, stirring constantly with a heat-resistant rubber spatula, taking care to
wipe the edges of the pan clean as you stir, until the mixture is thick and coats
the back of a spoon, about 2 minutes. Add the butter and stir until it's all
incorporated. Pour the sauce into the sauté pan with the onions. Mix well
and cook over medium-low heat for 5 minutes. This dish can be eaten warm
or at room temperature.

COOK'S TIP

This is even better when made with fresh petite pearl onions; however,
the peeling process can be quite an undertaking. The easiest method is to score
the bottom of each onion with a sharp knife and put them in boiling water for
1 minute. Drain well and literally squeeze them out of their skins. You will
need to parboil the fresh pearl onions for about 4 minutes before continuing
with the recipe.

As I have mentioned before, vegetables were considered as vile as
homework in the eyes of the Stellino
boys. However, this particular dish
was always welcome at our table
because of its winning sweet-and-sour

combination. It was usually served
with meat of some sort – lamb,
pork or beef – and prepared in large
quantities since we would often go
for seconds and thirds.

Now that I'm a responsible
adult, I still act as giddy as a young
child every time I'm presented with
this dish. In the presence of guests I
always show great restraint, however,
by limiting myself to a single serving –
a huge one, but single nevertheless.

This is a very easy vegetable dish with complex flavors. It was a favorite in our house, as I'm sure it will be in yours.

Serves 4

INGREDIENTS

2 tablespoons olive oil

4 tablespoons diced pancetta (Italian-style bacon)

4 tablespoons chopped onion

2 teaspoons chopped garlic

2 cups fresh or thawed frozen peas

1 teaspoon chopped fresh parsley

¼ teaspoon salt

¼ teaspoon pepper

¾ cup Chicken Stock (see page 139) or water

Put the olive oil and pancetta in a sauté pan and cook over medium heat until the pancetta begins to brown. Transfer the pancetta to another dish with a slotted spoon.

In the same pan, cook the onion and garlic over low heat until the onions are soft, about 4 minutes. Add the cooked pancetta, peas, chopped parsley, salt, pepper and chicken stock or water. Bring to a boil, then simmer until all the liquid is absorbed, about 10 minutes. The peas are now ready.

COOK'S TIP

If you are using fresh peas, you may want to increase the cooking time 5-10 minutes.

POMODORI GRATINATI

TOMATOES AU GRATIN

Serves 6

INGREDIENTS
6 Roma tomatoes
¾ teaspoon salt
2½ tablespoons olive oil
¼ teaspoon pepper
1½ tablespoons chopped garlic
2 tablespoons chopped fresh parsley
2 tablespoons Italian Bread Crumbs (see page 142)
2 tablespoons grated Romano or Parmigiano Reggiano cheese

Preheat the oven to 350° F.

Cut the tomatoes in half and squeeze out the seeds. Sprinkle with
½ teaspoon of the salt and turn them upside down on a rack to drain for 20
minutes. Place them on a broiling pan cut-side-up and brush with ¾ teaspoon
of the olive oil. Sprinkle with the remaining salt, the pepper, garlic, parsley,
bread crumbs and cheese. Brush lightly with the remaining olive oil and cook
in the preheated oven for 5 minutes. Brown lightly under the broiler and serve.

*This treatment dresses up the
common tomato, rendering it regal.
A feast with any kind of meat.*

BAKED TOMATOES STUFFED WITH RICE

When I was eight years old, Father introduced me to Rome, where he had spent his university years and where he met my mother. As a student in Rome, my father mastered the art of living on a strict budget. He made

it a point to seek out-of-the-way restaurants where princely feasts could be had at pauper's prices. The best of these was Cesaretto, a small, cave-like place, paneled in dark wood. Cesaretto, himself, recognized my father even after so many years of absence. "Sor Vincenzo, amvedi che sorpresa!" (Vincenzo, what a pleasant surprise), he yelled in his heavy Roman accent.

Serves 4

INGREDIENTS

4 firm tomatoes, about 8 ounces each
2¼ teaspoons + ¼ teaspoon salt
1 cup Chicken Stock (see page 139)
3 tablespoons olive oil
⅛ teaspoon red pepper flakes
1½ tablespoons chopped carrot
1½ tablespoons chopped onion
1½ tablespoons chopped celery
1 tablespoon chopped garlic
½ cup arborio rice
1 tablespoon chopped fresh parsley

Preheat the oven to 375° F.

Slice the tops off the tomatoes with a very sharp knife and set them aside. With a small paring knife, cut the tomato pulp away from the skin making sure you do not cut the skin. Using a tablespoon, scoop out the loosened pulp and set aside. Salt the insides of the tomatoes with 2¼ teaspoons of the salt, turn them upside down and let them drain.

Bring the stock to a boil in a small saucepan.

Heat 1½ tablespoons of the olive oil in a medium saucepan set on high heat until sizzling, about 1 minute. Add the red pepper flakes, carrot, onion and celery. Reduce the heat to low and cook for 5 minutes, stirring once. Add the chopped garlic and cook 1 minute more.

Raise the heat to high, add the rice and cook 2 minutes, stirring well to coat with the other ingredients. Add the chopped parsley and stir. Add the boiling stock and stir again. Cover the pot and simmer 10 minutes. Add the ¼ teaspoon of salt and ¾ tablespoon of the remaining olive oil to the rice, stir well.

Stuff the tomatoes with the rice mixture, being careful not to overstuff or they'll break as they cook.

Strain the juice that has accumulated from the tomato pulp you scooped out earlier. You should have about 6-8 tablespoons of juice. Pour the strained juice in equal parts over the stuffed tomatoes and cover with the tomato tops.

Brush the bottom of a nonstick pan and the tomatoes with the remaining olive oil. Place them in the oven and cook for 15 minutes. Cool the tomatoes to room temperature before you serve them. They always taste better the next day. Refrigerate them for up to 4 days, and let them come back to room temperature before serving.

He sat us at my father's old table in the back, close to the kitchen, where the smell of good food pervaded the air. Cesaretto then snapped his fingers and barked orders to his elderly waiters, who were dressed in long white aprons and black bow ties. Out of nowhere came a bounty of food, mostly small servings of various appetizers. The Tomatoes Stuffed with Rice stood out to my eyes and other senses. Mr. Cesaretto flatly denied my childlike request for the recipe so I've had to spend the intervening time perfecting my own version of this wonderful dish.

Let's raise a glass to Cesaretto, who started me on the quest. Sor Cesaretto ... Salute!

This dish makes me remember glorious roasts with lots of rich gravy. Garlic spikes the flavor into a new dimension, which in a "garliholic" family like ours was always a welcome addition. Mamma always made extra for the next day because there was no limit to the number of ways to mix and match this dish with other meals – we even liked it with sunny-side-up eggs!

There are several versions of this dish, each with a character of its own. The basic difference lies in the way the garlic is cooked.

Serves 4 to 6

INGREDIENTS

2 pounds russet potatoes, peeled and quartered
1 head garlic, broken into individual peeled cloves
⅛ teaspoon garlic powder (optional)
¾ teaspoon salt
¼ teaspoon pepper
¾ teaspoon Aromat (Knorr Aromatic Salt, either chicken or meat base)
3 tablespoons grated Parmigiano Reggiano cheese
¼ cup heavy cream

Put the potatoes and garlic into a large saucepan with enough cold water to cover by 2 inches. Cover the pot and bring to a boil. Once the water reaches a boil, uncover, reduce the heat to medium-low and cook for 15-20 minutes, until the potatoes and the garlic cloves are so soft they will break with pressure from the back of a spoon. Drain well and return the garlic and potatoes to the saucepan. Mash the potato mixture well, add all the other ingredients except the cream and mix with a sturdy, wooden spoon.

Place the saucepan over medium-low heat and add the cream, stirring continuously until it is incorporated. Turn off the heat and serve.

COOK'S TIPS

Here are two other versions of this recipe:

With Roasted Garlic

Slice the top ⅓ off two large heads of garlic, brush with 1 tablespoon of olive oil and place the sliced top back on. Place the garlic in a ramekin, cover with aluminum foil and bake in a 400° F oven for 35 minutes. When cool enough to handle, squeeze out the garlic pulp. You can do this patiently, one clove at a time, or the whole head at once. Add the garlic pulp to the mashed potatoes and continue with the original recipe.

With Garlic Roasted in Oil

Add the peeled cloves from 1 head of garlic to 2 cups of simmering olive oil. Simmer gently for 30 minutes, until the garlic cloves are completely cooked and very soft. Surprise – you've just made garlic olive oil! Add the soft cloves to the mashed potatoes and continue with the original recipe.

There is no better accompaniment for roast meat or barbecued steak than a large tray of roasted potatoes. The following recipe is one that Nonna Maria passed on to my mother. I can still remember placing our large trays of potatoes in the wood-burning oven and smelling the magic of the flavors coming together. I guarantee you that it will feel like a day in the country every time you make this potato dish for your family or guests – even without a wood-burning stove.

Serves 4

INGREDIENTS

3 pounds russet potatoes, peeled and thickly sliced
1½ large heads garlic, unpeeled
1 teaspoon salt
½ teaspoon pepper
2½ tablespoons chopped fresh rosemary
6½ tablespoons olive oil
1 small white onion, thinly sliced

Preheat the oven to 425° F.

Place the potatoes and garlic in a large pot and cover with water. Cover the pot and bring to a boil. Uncover, reduce the heat to medium and cook for 10 minutes. The potatoes should still be a bit hard. Drain. Transfer the garlic cloves to a glass of cold water. When they are cool enough to handle, peel them by simply squeezing them out of their softened skins.

Place the potatoes and peeled garlic in a large bowl. Sprinkle with the salt, pepper, rosemary and 4½ tablespoons of the olive oil and mix well.

Grease the bottom of a large baking sheet with the remaining 2 tablespoons of olive oil. Place the potatoes on the baking sheet and roast for 20 minutes, turning once. Spread the sliced onion on top of the potatoes and roast until the potatoes are well browned, about 20 minutes more, turning once. If you like them extra crispy, cook 10 minutes more.

COOK'S TIP

If you're making this potato dish together with roasted meat, mix 3 tablespoons of the defatted roasting juices into the potatoes during the last 5 minutes of cooking. Serve proudly alongside your roast.

P O T A T O   C O I N S

Serves 4

INGREDIENTS

4 (6-ounce) new white potatoes
4 tablespoons olive oil
½ teaspoon salt
⅛ teaspoon pepper
4 garlic cloves, chopped
2 tablespoons chopped fresh parsley
1½ tablespoons butter

This is a truly simple recipe that brings out the best in the humble potato. Trust me when I say potato coins will enrich your menus. You can serve them with any kind of meat or fish.

Do not peel the potatoes. Cut them in half lengthwise, then cut them in slices as thick as a quarter.

Heat the oil in a 12-inch nonstick pan set on high heat until sizzling, about 2 minutes. Add the potato slices and cook for 8 minutes, stirring every 2 minutes to ensure that they brown evenly without sticking or burning. Be very careful not to burn the potatoes during this stage. Reduce the heat to medium. Add ⅛ teaspoon of the salt and the pepper and cook 10 more minutes, stirring occasionally. Add the remaining salt, the garlic and parsley and cook for 5 minutes. Add the butter and cook for 5 minutes, stirring occasionally.

COOK'S TIP

While cooking, the potatoes will shrink in size and some of them will stick together. Don't worry – that's the look of this dish.

STEWED POTATOES

A great side dish with any kind of meat or fish, these potatoes are also a fantastic meal when served with a small salad and good Italian bread. It is also light enough to use as an appetizer course.

Serves 4

INGREDIENTS
3 tablespoons olive oil
1 large onion, chopped
4 garlic cloves, sliced
1 small branch fresh rosemary (about 3 inches)
¼ teaspoon red pepper flakes
3 large russet potatoes, peeled and cut into 1-inch cubes
1 (1-pound) can peeled Italian tomatoes
½ chicken bouillon cube
2 tablespoons chopped fresh Italian parsley
½ teaspoon salt (optional)

Cook the oil, onion, garlic, rosemary and red pepper flakes in a 10-inch sauté pan over medium heat until the onion is translucent, about 5 minutes, stirring occasionally to prevent sticking. Add the potatoes, stir well and cook for 3 minutes.

Pour the tomatoes and their juices into a bowl and break the tomatoes into pieces. Stir the tomatoes, their juices and the bouillon cube into the potatoes and bring to a boil. Reduce the heat and simmer with the cover slightly ajar for 35 minutes.

Add the parsley and salt (if you wish), stir gently, raise the heat to medium and cook uncovered until the potatoes are tender, about 15 minutes. Serve immediately or let the flavors meld overnight.

COOK'S TIP
Use the kind of potato that is best for the region of the world in which you live, but remember, different potatoes will have different cooking times.

FRITTELLE DI PANE

BREAD FRITTERS

Serves 4 to 6

INGREDIENTS

4 eggs

6 tablespoons Italian Bread Crumbs (see page 142)

4 tablespoons grated Parmigiano Reggiano cheese

4 tablespoons grated provolone or Romano cheese

¼ teaspoon salt

¼ teaspoon pepper

6 tablespoons olive oil

In a large bowl, mix the eggs, bread crumbs, Parmigiano Reggiano cheese, provolone, salt and pepper.

Heat half the oil in a large sauté pan set on medium-high heat until sizzling, about 2 minutes. When the oil is ready, reduce the heat to medium. Carefully spoon generous tablespoons of the bread mixture (about 6 or 8) into the hot pan. Flatten each cake slightly with the back of your spoon and fry for about 1½ minutes on each side. They cook quickly and rise slightly during cooking. Transfer the cakes to a plate lined with paper towels to drain off the excess oil. Repeat the process until all the batter is cooked. The fritters are delicious hot from the pan or reheated in the oven the next day.

My mother and grandmother are perfect examples of my theory that the cornerstone of every gourmet tradition lies in the inventiveness of self-reliant housewives. These delicious frittelle obviously originated in some such housewife's desire to use old bread. They make a quick and easy side dish, but served hot on a bed of tomato sauce topped with melted provolone, they achieve gourmet status.

Stuffing, in my modest opinion, is an unsung hero of the Italian culinary tradition. I'm always amazed at how such a simple assembly of ingredients can produce such tasty results. Stuffing can

elevate even the most humble cut of meat or the most common vegetable to greatness.

While they may not be the ultimate or the most traditional recipes, the following three versions of my stuffing have afforded me the respect and admiration of my cooking colleagues and the inner satisfaction of a job well done.

I use this stuffing in Stuffed Pork Chops (see page 74) and Stuffed Peppers (see page 13).

Makes 2 to 2½ cups

INGREDIENTS
2 tablespoons olive oil
½ red onion, finely chopped
4 garlic cloves, sliced
⅛ teaspoon red pepper flakes
¾ pound white button mushrooms, sliced
1 bay leaf
¾ cup white wine
1 (14½-ounce) can stewed tomatoes
1 tablespoon chopped fresh parsley
1 tablespoon chopped fresh basil
1 large egg
¾ cup Italian Bread Crumbs (see page 142)
½ cup grated Romano cheese

Pour the olive oil into a nonstick sauté pan and cook the onions over medium-low heat until soft, about 3 minutes. Add the garlic and red pepper flakes and continue cooking for 5 minutes. Increase the heat to high, add the sliced mushrooms and the bay leaf and cook 2 minutes longer, stirring well to prevent sticking. Add the wine and cook until it has all evaporated, 3 more minutes.

Drain the stewed tomatoes and reserve their juices. Chop the tomatoes roughly, add them to the sauté pan, reduce the heat to medium and cook for 2 minutes. Add the parsley and the basil, stirring well. Pour in the juice of the stewed tomatoes and cook over medium-low heat for 5 minutes, stirring occasionally. The mixture should be fairly thick and almost dry. If it is very watery, cook for 3 minutes more.

Transfer the mixture to a large mixing bowl. Add the egg, bread crumbs and cheese. Mix until it is all incorporated. The stuffing should be very thick and fairly moist. If it is still watery add more cheese and bread crumbs.

FARCITO CON LE SALSICCIE

S A U S A G E   S T U F F I N G

Makes 2½ to 3 cups

INGREDIENTS
2 tablespoons olive oil
10 ounces hot Italian sausage, removed from the casing
1 white onion, finely chopped
4 garlic cloves, sliced
⅛ teaspoon red pepper flakes
¾ pound mushrooms, finely sliced
1 bay leaf
¾ cup white wine
1 (14½-ounce) can stewed tomatoes
1 tablespoon chopped fresh parsley
1 tablespoon chopped fresh basil
2 eggs
1 cup Italian Bread Crumbs (see page 142)
¾ cup grated Romano cheese

This meat-based stuffing is great in bell peppers or tomatoes as a main course. See my Stuffed Peppers (see page 13) and Stuffed Pork Chops (see page 74) for examples.

Pour the oil into a nonstick sauté pan set on medium heat and brown the sausage for 3 minutes. Transfer the sausage to a plate and set aside.

Discard all but 3 tablespoons of the fat left in the sauté pan. On medium heat, cook the onion for 3 minutes. Add the garlic and red pepper flakes, reduce the heat to low and cook for 5 minutes. Increase the heat to high, add the sliced mushrooms and bay leaf, stir well and cook 2 minutes. Add the wine and cook until it has almost evaporated, about 3 minutes.

Drain the tomatoes, reserving the juices separately. Roughly chop the tomatoes and add them to the sauté pan. Reduce the heat to medium and cook 2 minutes. Add the parsley, basil, reserved tomato juices and sausage, stir well, and cook 5 minutes, stirring occasionally. The mixture should be fairly thick and almost dry. If it is very watery, cook 3 minutes more. Transfer the mixture to a large mixing bowl.

Add the cooked sausage, the eggs, bread crumbs and cheese and mix well. The stuffing should be very thick and fairly moist. If it is still watery, add more cheese and bread crumbs to your taste.

The following recipe shows the versatility of this stuffing mixture. When it is baked like this, the stuffing becomes an excellent substitute for mashed potatoes, as well as a fantastic savory side dish for any entree.

Serves 4 to 6

INGREDIENTS

2 tablespoons olive oil

10 ounces hot Italian sausage, removed from the casing (optional)

1 white onion, finely chopped

4 garlic cloves, sliced

⅛ teaspoon red pepper flakes

¾ pound mushrooms, finely sliced

1 bay leaf

¾ cup white wine

1 (14½-ounce) can stewed tomatoes

1 tablespoon chopped fresh parsley

1 tablespoon chopped fresh basil

3 eggs

1½ cups Italian Bread Crumbs (see page 142)

¾ cup grated Romano cheese

Preheat the oven to 350° F.

Pour the oil into a nonstick sauté pan and brown the sausage over medium heat, about 3 minutes. Set aside. Discard all but 3 tablespoons of the fat left in the sauté pan. Sauté the onion in the reserved fat for 3 minutes over medium heat. Add the garlic and red pepper flakes to the pan, reduce the heat to low and cook 5 minutes. Increase the heat to high, add the sliced mushrooms and bay leaf, stir well and cook 2 minutes. Add the wine and cook until it has all evaporated, 3 minutes.

Drain the stewed tomatoes and reserve their juices. Roughly chop the tomatoes and add them to the sauté pan. Reduce the heat to medium and cook 2 minutes. Add the parsley and basil and toss well. Add the juices from the stewed tomatoes and cook over medium-low heat for 5 minutes, stirring occasionally. The mixture should be fairly thick and almost dry. If it is very watery, cook for 3 minutes more. Transfer the mixture to a large mixing bowl.

Separate the egg whites and yolks. Add the yolks to the stuffing mixture along with 1 cup of the bread crumbs and the cheese. Beat the egg whites until they have almost a meringue-like consistency. Fold them into the stuffing.

Coat the bottom and sides of individual baking ramekins or a small baking dish with butter, coat well with the remaining bread crumbs and fill with the stuffing mixture. Bake in the preheated oven for 20–25 minutes. Run a sharp paring knife around the edges of the ramekins to loosen the stuffing. Turn the ramekins upside down over each dinner plate and the baked mixture will slide right out.

DOLCI

Desserts

SFOGLIATA DI MELE

APPLE TART

Serves 4

INGREDIENTS
1 (12-inch) circle puff pastry, thawed
3 apples, peeled, cored and thinly sliced
3 tablespoons sugar
3 tablespoons butter, thinly sliced
2 tablespoons powdered sugar

Preheat the oven to 475° F.

Place the pastry on a greased baking sheet. Arrange the apples on top in a spiral design, leaving a 1-inch border all around. Sprinkle with the sugar and scatter with the butter pieces. Bake in the preheated oven until the puff pastry rises and the edges of the apples are slightly charred, about 10 to 15 minutes. Remove from the oven and dust with the powdered sugar.

COOK'S TIP
To heighten the flavor, brush the top of the cooked tart with 3 tablespoons of melted apple jelly and then dust with the powdered sugar.

I remember this recipe as a particularly delicious dessert cooked to perfection in the wood oven of my grandmother's house. It is easy to prepare at the last minute and still great tasting, even without a wood oven.

If you can't find frozen puff pastry in a circle shape, just put a few squares together and roll them into a large one to cut out a 12-inch circle.

FRAGOLE ALLO ZABAGLIONE

STRAWBERRY ZABAGLIONE

"**P**er chi é sto zabaglione?" (Who needs this zabaglione?)

This is a common joke among young Italian men because zabaglione has been known since the old times for strengthening the passionate stamina of young men in love. While I'm sorry to say it never helped me in that way, I'm happy to certify that it always cures my heartaches (but then again, so has a good plate of pasta!).

Experiment a few times before you attempt this for guests. The egg thickening process is a bit tricky, but it's like riding a bicycle – once you learn, you'll never forget. You can also substitute Champagne for Marsala wine, which makes it just a bit fluffier – the bubbles, you know!

And who knows: you might unexpectedly find within yourself the vigor and passion of a young Casanova.

Serves 4

INGREDIENTS
1 pound strawberries, hulled and sliced
6 tablespoons dry Marsala wine
4 egg yolks
4 tablespoons sugar
4 mint leaves, for decoration

Place the strawberries in a bowl, mix with 2 tablespoons of the Marsala and set aside.

In the top half of a double boiler, whisk the egg yolks and sugar to a creamy consistency. In the bottom half of the double boiler, bring a small amount of water to a boil. Place the egg mixture on top, making sure it doesn't touch the water, and beat well until it starts to thicken, about 5 minutes. Be careful not to beat too long and cook the eggs. Remove from the heat and stir in the remaining Marsala wine, whisking until well incorporated. Return to the top of the double boiler and whisk until thickened, 3-5 minutes. Remove from the heat and set aside.

Divide the strawberries among four wine glasses and top with the zabaglione cream. It can be eaten warm or placed in the refrigerator and eaten cold later. Decorate with a mint leaf before serving.

COOK'S TIP
If you don't have a double boiler, you can just boil water in a saucepan and hold the egg mixture in a bowl over the boiling water while you whisk.

FRAGOLE DELLA MAMMA

MAMMA'S STRAWBERRIES

Serves 4

INGREDIENTS
1½ pounds strawberries, sliced
¼ cup sugar
½ cup dry Marsala or white wine
1 tablespoon chopped fresh mint

In a large mixing bowl, combine all the ingredients, making sure the strawberries are well coated with the sugar. Cover with plastic wrap and refrigerate for 4 hours to allow the flavors to meld. It's delicious plain, or spooned over pieces of pound cake with a dollop of whipped cream.

COOK'S TIP
One small variation: In a small saucepan, mix 1½ teaspoons cornstarch with 1½ cups of orange juice and bring to a boil, stirring until thickened. Stir in the ¼ cup of sugar until it dissolves, then remove from the heat and set aside. When at room temperature, fold in the strawberries and the wine. This gives you a thicker sauce and more complex flavors.

In the summer, my mother often took Mario and me to the beach. This recipe was a delicious little dessert that she would assemble in the morning and we would all enjoy at lunch. Whenever I make it, I can see Mario and me running around the beach in Mother Nature's bathing suit, squealing, laughing, and splashing.

STRAWBERRIES IN BALSAMIC VINEGAR

The first time I enjoyed this simple dessert, I was 20 years old, traveling in Modena with my father. The restaurant we ate at was good but nothing spectacular. Of course, you must keep in mind that with two

diners like my father and me, nothing shy of a miracle earned our nod of approval.

When it came to dessert, the waiter suggested the house specialty, Strawberries in Balsamic Vinegar. Father and I looked at each other, incredulous. After all, who had ever heard of vinegar for dessert? To this day I'm glad I ventured into the unknown and discovered this simple and delicious treat.

I'd like to credit my mother with the addition of the mint, which, in my humble opinion completes the dish in a very satisfying way.

Serves 4

INGREDIENTS
1½ pounds strawberries, quartered
2 tablespoons sugar
¾ tablespoon chopped fresh mint
2 tablespoons balsamic vinegar

Place the strawberries in a large bowl and sprinkle with the sugar. Add the mint and vinegar and mix well. Let the mixture rest for 1 hour before serving.

COOK'S TIP
For sharper sweet and sour contrasts, cook 3 tablespoons of balsamic vinegar and 3 tablespoons of sugar in a small nonstick saucepan until reduced by one third. Pour over the strawberries, add the mint, mix well and enjoy!

PESCHE MERINGATE

PEACHES IN MERINGUE

Serves 6

INGREDIENTS

3 egg whites

3 tablespoons sugar

3 medium peaches, fresh or canned, halved, pitted and peeled

3 Amaretti cookies, crumbled

2 tablespoons rum or cassis

¾ cup peach juice or the syrup from the canned peaches

1 tablespoon butter

Preheat the oven to 450° F.

Place the egg whites in a metal bowl and beat with an electric mixer until frothy. Slowly beat in the sugar, until it becomes a glossy, white and thick meringue.

Place the peach halves in a small ovenproof baking dish and sprinkle with the crumbled cookies and rum or cassis. Put a spoonful of the meringue on each peach half. Pour the juice or syrup in the bottom of the dish and bake until the meringue just starts to brown, about 5 minutes.

Transfer the peach halves to small dessert bowls. Add the butter to the cooking liquid in the baking dish, mix well and divide the sauce among the dessert bowls.

The Signora Lidia was the owner and operator of a small restaurant. She didn't possess the most charming of personalities – in truth, she was a bit of a gruff old maid. But she did make the most incredible desserts and that was enough to make her restaurant the place that my teammates and I used to visit after our basketball games.

Anyway, on the eve of my departure for America, Signora Lidia came to a little farewell party that my teammates had organized for me. I was quite surprised when she came over to give me a hug and a little envelope. I was so shocked by her sincere display of emotion that I put the envelope in my jacket pocket and didn't open it until the next day. It contained the recipe for my favorite dessert from her restaurant: Pesche Meringate.

Signora Lidia, Grazie!

ZUCCOTTO MERINGATO AL FORNO

BAKED ICE CREAM CAKE

Serves 6 to 8

INGREDIENTS

2 (10-ounce) frozen pound cakes
9 tablespoons Amaretto liqueur
1 quart French vanilla ice cream, softened
3 egg whites
2 tablespoons sugar

What follows is a fabulous demonstration of how to turn a simple selection of common, commercially packaged ingredients into a delicacy fit for a banquet. Don't think of this as cheating, but as an example of boundless creativity in action.

Okay, call it what you will; but the fact remains: this simple dessert looks spectacular and tastes even better!

The day before serving, line a small bowl (about 8 inches wide and 2½ inches deep) with plastic wrap, leaving a 3-inch overhang around the edges.

Cut one whole pound cake, and ¼ of the other into ¼-inch slices. Save the leftover pound cake for other uses. Line the inside of the prepared bowl completely with the cake slices, pushing down to mold them to the bowl shape. Break up a couple of the slices to fill any small holes in the cake lining. Drizzle with 3 tablespoons of the Amaretto. Fill the bottom half with half of the ice cream, pushing down firmly with a large spoon. Cover with a layer of cake slices and sprinkle with 3 more tablespoons of the Amaretto. Cover with the remaining ice cream, pushing down firmly with a large spoon. Cover with a layer of cake slices and sprinkle with the remaining Amaretto. Fold over the plastic wrap to cover the top and place in the freezer overnight to harden. It will keep for up to 2 weeks.

Just before serving, preheat the oven to 450° F. In a small bowl, beat the egg whites with an electric mixer until frothy. Add the sugar and beat until the meringue forms stiff peaks and has a shiny gloss, about 3-5 minutes. Transfer to a pastry bag.

Remove the cake from the freezer and unmold onto an ovenproof serving dish. Remove the plastic and pipe the meringue over the entire surface. Bake in the hot oven until the meringue is just golden brown, about 5 minutes.

OTTO, OTTO E OTTO

RICOTTA TART

Serves 8 to 10

INGREDIENTS

8 eggs, separated
8 tablespoons sugar
2 pounds ricotta cheese
8 tablespoons all-purpose flour
½ cup semisweet chocolate chips
zest from 1 medium orange, finely chopped

Preheat the oven to 400° F.

Grease and flour a 9-inch springform pan with a mixture of flour and sugar, tapping out the excess.

In a large bowl, beat the egg yolks and 4 tablespoons of the sugar with an electric mixer until the yolks form pale yellow ribbons when you lift the beaters, about 5 minutes.

In a large bowl, beat the egg whites and the remaining 4 tablespoons of sugar with an electric mixer until shiny and doubled in volume, about 5 minutes. Do not overbeat or they will dry out.

In a large bowl, mix the ricotta cheese, beaten egg yolks, and the flour until it forms a smooth paste. Fold in the beaten egg whites, chocolate chips, and orange zest. Spoon into the prepared pan, reduce the oven heat to 325° F and bake for 1-1½ hours or until a knife blade inserted in the cake comes out clean. If it needs further cooking, cook in additional increments of 10 minutes until done. Let it cool to room temperature before serving.

It is normal for this tart to crack, so don't be alarmed when this happens.

COOK'S TIP

If you've never tried fresh ricotta cheese, this recipe is a good excuse to call an Italian deli and give it a try. As a child, we had an arrangement with a sheepherder who rented land from my father: he paid us in fresh cheeses and milk – an arrangement that I felt was excellent, when it resulted in this dessert. I know you'll love it, too.

I was (and still am) totally in love with this recipe for my father's ricotta tart. Translated the name means "eight, eight and eight" and comes from the fact that the ingredients are all in multiples of eight.

But the most important aspect of this recipe is the fact that it's the only one my father and I can cook together without arguing about ingredients or alternative cooking methods. To us it is a symbol of complete understanding. As you can imagine, the two of us are very opinionated individuals with many diverging views on love, work, politics and life in general. Destiny has challenged us with many trials and tribulations, but even at our most difficult moments I can always look him in the eyes and say, "otto, otto e otto." Then his face works its way to a wide smile and he says, "Va bene" (okay).

Sometimes it is difficult just to say "I love you," I guess more for some than for others. But when it comes to my dad and me, we are always able to tell each other, "otto, otto e otto."

This was one of our favorite Christmas desserts. Mario and I, usually rambunctious rascals, would stand quietly on chairs pushed against the table, watching my mother's every move. I remember her, smiling, describing each task and letting us taste a spoonful at each stage to teach us about the proper mix and consistency. To Mario and me, it held all the delights of an unfolding magic show.

The grand finale was when my mother gave us permission to clean the mixing bowl. This was an activity that Mario and I undertook with a sense of friendly competition and ruthless abandon. The end result was a clean bowl and mascarpone cheese all over our faces, clothes and hair. I remember my mother standing over us, laughing softly with her long hand over her mouth.

I'm happy to report that my enthusiasm for this childhood bowl-cleaning ritual is something I've carried into my adult life. My wife watches with great delight as I lose my dignified professional demeanor and dig into the mixing bowl, covering my beard and clothes with mascarpone cheese.

Of course, the mixing bowl can be cleaned simply by washing it, but sometime when you're alone, let yourself go!

T I R A M I S Ù
" P I C K - M E - U P " C A K E

Serves 6 to 8

INGREDIENTS
14 ounces savoiardi or ladyfingers
2 cups strong coffee
⅓ cup coffee liqueur
8 eggs, separated
1½ cups sugar
1 teaspoon vanilla
1 pound + 1½ ounces mascarpone cheese
¼ pound finely grated semisweet chocolate

The day before serving, lay all the cookies out on a baking sheet and brush them on both sides with the coffee and coffee liqueur. They should be moist on the outside but still crunchy on the inside.

In a bowl, beat the egg yolks, ¾ cup of the sugar and the vanilla with an electric mixer until the mixture is thick enough to form a long ribbon when you lift the beaters, about 5 minutes. Add the mascarpone cheese, beat for 3 minutes then set aside.

Clean the beaters of the electric mixer carefully and in a clean bowl, beat the egg whites with the remaining sugar until they form stiff peaks and have a glossy sheen, about 5 minutes.

Fold the egg whites into the mascarpone mixture, ⅓ at a time. Be careful: if you don't fold it in completely, you'll have a coarse texture. Be sure you fold the egg whites in rather than stirring them as this will cause the dessert to lose its lightness.

In a 9 x 17-inch glass baking dish, assemble the dessert. Layer half the cookies on the bottom, top with half the cream and half the grated chocolate. Repeat with one more layer of each. Place the dish, uncovered, in the refrigerator, overnight.

The next day it is ready to be served.

COOK'S TIP
To grate the chocolate, use the largest holes of a cheese grater, what's commonly called the shredder side.

BIANCO MANGIARE

MILK PUDDING WITH ALMONDS

Serves 7

INGREDIENTS
6 tablespoons cornstarch
3 cups milk
½ cup + 2 tablespoons sugar
¼ teaspoon grated lemon zest
¼ cup chopped almonds or candied fruit
½ cup grated or chopped semisweet chocolate

I remember this recipe as one of my family's favorite desserts – simple preparation with surprisingly great results. The almonds give it a distinctive flavor which is common to many Sicilian desserts.

In a small bowl, mix the cornstarch and 1 cup of the milk until smooth.

In a 2-quart, heavy-bottom saucepan on medium heat, cook the remaining 2 cups of milk and the sugar until it reaches a soft boil. Add the lemon zest, almonds or candied fruit, and cornstarch-milk mixture and cook until thickened, stirring continuously, about 5 minutes. Remove from the heat and let sit for 3 minutes, stirring to prevent sticking.

Pour into small dessert cups and cool for 10 minutes. Top with the grated or chopped chocolate and place in the refrigerator, uncovered, until ready to serve. Serve cold.

COOK'S TIP
If you like a perfectly smooth pudding, replace the almonds with 1 teaspoon of almond extract. You can spike this dessert by adding 2-4 tablespoons of almond liqueur to the thickened pudding before pouring it into the dessert cups.

My grandmother, Nonna Adele, seemed like a small frail woman, but her strength and determination carried her through two world wars. I was told she had been beautiful once, but a series of tragic events, stories that were always censored to protect my young ears, had taken its toll.

Still, her smile promised better times ahead; and her style of cooking, while frugal, was ebullient with strong flavors which populate my nostalgic recollections of times gone by. The following recipe is her's from the time during World War II. Humble ingredients – stale bread, milk and eggs – transformed as if by magic.

I would watch her, enchanted, perched at the kitchen table. Nonna's bony fingers seemed to have a life of their own, moving rapidly, cutting and mixing while she hummed a tune. Occasionally she would smile and give me a bit of chocolate to munch. Every time I make this recipe I can feel her close.

Ciao, Nonna!

Serves 8 to 10

INGREDIENTS

8 cups day-old bread, cut into cubes
(use any hearty white, sourdough, or challah)
½ cup semisweet chocolate chips
3 eggs
3 egg yolks
½ cup sugar
2 cups milk
1 cup heavy cream
½ teaspoon vanilla

Preheat the oven to 375° F. Grease a 9 x 13-inch baking dish.

In a large bowl, mix the bread cubes and chocolate chips and spoon into the prepared baking dish.

In the same bowl, beat the eggs, egg yolks and the sugar with an electric mixer until it forms a thick yellow custard. Add the milk, cream and vanilla and beat for 3 minutes. Pour the custard over the bread and chocolate, pushing the bread down until it's submerged in the liquid as much as possible. Let rest in the refrigerator for 30 minutes. Reduce the oven heat to 350° F and bake the pudding for 30 minutes or until a knife blade inserted in the center comes out clean. Remove from the oven and serve at room temperature.

You might as well forget about counting calories and just make a swan dive into this divine mixture of heavenly flavors. Enjoy every bite, then loosen your belt and go for seconds.

COOK'S TIP

If you don't like the top of your pudding brown, loosely cover the top of the pan with aluminum foil during the baking process. This will also make the pudding more moist.

SUGHI E BRODI
—————◆—————
Sauces & Stocks

S U G O   D I   P O M O D O R O

T O M A T O   S A U C E

Makes 5¾ cups

INGREDIENTS
4 tablespoons olive oil
4 whole garlic cloves
¾ cup finely chopped onions
2 (28-ounce) cans peeled Italian tomatoes
10 fresh basil leaves

Pour the oil into a 3-quart pot set on medium-high heat and cook the garlic and onions for 3 minutes. Reduce the heat to a simmer and cook until the onions are soft and start to brown, about 10 minutes, stirring occasionally.

While the onions are cooking, put the tomatoes and their juice in a blender or food processor and puree until smooth. Add the tomato puree to the onion mixture, raise the heat to high and bring to a boil for 5-8 minutes. Reduce the heat, add the basil and simmer for 25 minutes, stirring occasionally.

COOK'S TIPS
I can't stress enough the importance of using Italian tomatoes. They are naturally sweeter than their American counterparts. If you have to use American tomatoes, double the amount of chopped onions and add 2 more tablespoons of oil.

Remember, this is a plain, unsalted sauce, which is great as an ingredient in other finished sauces. If you want to use this as a garnish for your pasta, I'd suggest you add ¼ teaspoon of salt for each 2 cups, according to your taste.

This recipe is a simple and efficient way to prepare a basic sauce that can be used for all the recipes in this book.

For the Stellino family, the last two weekends in June were dedicated exclusively to visiting tomato farms, scouting "conserva." This "oro rosso" (red gold) was bottles of crushed ripe tomatoes that became the base for tomato sauce.

My father's favorite territory was in the province of Trapani. We would buy cases of conserva from the farmers, then start home, our small car loaded with our bounty. Sometimes my father stopped by the side of the road. He would hold my hand while we both leaned against the car to watch the last flash of sunlight disappear into the sea and tell me about a magic land on the other side of the horizon. A special place where the sun is always warm, the ocean is always full of fish and dreams come true ... California.

Today, living in my Los Angeles home, I watch the sun set behind the crested waves of the Pacific Ocean and sometimes, I wave to the little boy and his father, standing by the side of the road with their tomato sauce, in a faraway land on the other side of the horizon. It's a place that shines with the beauty of romantic recollection.

"Ciao, Papá."

Each of the Italian regions has a version or two of this sauce in their culinary tradition. My version always reminds me of John Wayne!

As a child I was a passionate fan of American cowboy movies. I particularly liked the dining scenes, when cowboys would sit around the campfire sipping coffee, eating a red delicacy from their blue and white speckled dishes. I never knew exactly what that red stuff was but I assumed it was Italian meat sauce. My brother and I considered it most exciting to sit down at the dinner table with our cowboy hats and trusty toy six-shooters packed in our side holsters and eat meat sauce like John Wayne.

It was with great sorrow many years later that I discovered that John Wayne wasn't Italian and he wasn't eating Italian meat sauce by the campfire. It was chili! Oh well.

Serves 4 to 6

INGREDIENTS

5 tablespoons olive oil
¼ teaspoon red pepper flakes
½ cup finely chopped celery
½ cup finely chopped carrots
½ cup finely chopped onions
4 garlic cloves, sliced
1 large bay leaf
1 tablespoon chopped fresh sage
2 tablespoons chopped fresh basil
2 ounces finely diced prosciutto
¼ pound ground veal
¼ pound ground lamb
¼ pound ground beef
⅓ cup red wine
½ cup Tomato Sauce (see page 137)
2 tablespoons tomato paste
2 cups Chicken or Beef Stock (see pages 139 and 140)
salt and black pepper, to taste

Heat the oil in a large saucepan set on high heat for 1 minute. Add the red pepper flakes, celery, carrots, onions, garlic, bay leaf, sage and basil and cook for 2 minutes, stirring continuously. Reduce the heat to medium-low and cook 10 minutes more, stirring occasionally.

Raise the heat to high, add the prosciutto, veal, lamb and beef and cook, stirring continuously, for 2 minutes. Add the wine, reduce the heat to medium and let it cook until almost evaporated, about 5 minutes. Raise the heat to high, add the tomato sauce, tomato paste and stock and bring to a boil. Reduce the heat to a simmer, cover the pot and cook for 45 minutes, stirring twice.

If you like your sauce thicker, remove the cover during the last 15 minutes of cooking. Taste for salt and pepper.

BRODO DI POLLO

CHICKEN STOCK

Makes 2 quarts

INGREDIENTS

1 (3-pound) whole chicken, without the liver

2 small carrots, peeled and quartered

2 celery ribs, cut into 2-inch pieces

2 white onions, quartered

1 small fresh rosemary branch, about 4 inches, *or* ½ teaspoon dried

3 sprigs fresh parsley

10 leaves fresh basil

3 sprigs fresh thyme *or* ½ teaspoon dried

1 tablespoon whole black peppercorns

2 eggs, beaten well, with their shells

1 cup white wine

¾ tablespoon salt

3¼ quarts water

Place all the ingredients in a large stockpot and bring to a boil. Reduce the heat and simmer, with the cover slightly ajar, for 2 hours. Skim any foam that rises to the top every 30 minutes.

Remove the chicken. Strain the stock through a fine sieve lined with cheesecloth. Once the stock comes to room temperature, place it in the refrigerator overnight. All the fat will rise to the top, harden and become solid white. Skim it off and discard.

The stock will keep up to 4 days in the refrigerator and for 1 month frozen.

I must confess that early in life I was not what you'd call an afficionado of chicken stock – I was a spaghetti and tomato sauce man. We Sicilian cowboys need a he-man meal when we come galloping home from a day

out on the prairie.

On the other hand, chicken stock was always the prescription for the occasional illnesses that afflict every growing cowboy all over the world. I thought of it as a "girly" kind of food, but all that changed when my Aunt Buliti convinced me that John Wayne always ate chicken soup when he was sick.

BRODO DI CARNE
BEEF STOCK

"Un buon brodo é il segreto del cuoco"
(a good stock is the chef's secret).

    Making a good beef stock is
very simple – don't let it intimidate
you. I invite you all to try my version –
surely you won't be disappointed.

Yields 2 quarts

INGREDIENTS

5 pounds beef or veal bones, preferably shin bones
3 tablespoons tomato paste
1 tablespoon all-purpose flour
1 large carrot, cut into 1-inch pieces
1 large onion, quartered
1 large celery rib, cut into 1-inch pieces
1 teaspoon whole black peppercorns
5 whole cloves
2 bay leaves
1½ teaspoons dried thyme *or* 2 fresh sprigs
5 sprigs fresh basil
5 fresh sage leaves
2 sprigs fresh rosemary, about 3 inches each
1 gallon water

Preheat the oven to 400° F. Place the bones in a large ovenproof pan and bake until well browned, turning twice, 20-30 minutes. Remove from the oven.

In a large bowl, mix the tomato paste, flour, carrot, onion and celery. Spoon this mixture on top of the browned bones and roast in the oven for 15 minutes.

While the bones are cooking, make a cheesecloth pouch and place all the spices and herbs inside. Tie it securely with kitchen twine and put at the bottom of a large stockpot.

Transfer the cooked vegetables and bones into the stockpot with the pouch of herbs. Be careful not to pour in the fat that has accumulated in the bottom of the pan. Cover with the water, bring to a boil, reduce the heat to a simmer and cook for 6-8 hours, without stirring. Check the water level. When you see that it is reduced by ⅓ (about halfway through the simmering), add 3 cups of fresh water.

Strain the stock, discarding the bones and vegetables. Let come to room temperature then refrigerate overnight. The next day, discard any of the fat that has congealed on the top. You can refrigerate the stock for up to 5 days. It will keep frozen for up to 1 month.

BRODETTO DI GAMBERI

S H R I M P   S T O C K

Makes 2½ cups

INGREDIENTS

2 tablespoons olive oil

shells from 1 pound raw shrimp

2 whole garlic cloves

1½ tablespoons chopped onion

1½ tablespoons chopped celery

1½ tablespoons chopped carrot

1 tablespoon tomato paste

1 tablespoon chopped fresh parsley

1 teaspoon thyme

¼ cup white wine

4 cups clam juice

¼ teaspoon salt

¼ teaspoon pepper

Fresh shrimp was always considered a special treat at our table. We tried not to waste anything, even the shells. The following recipe uses shrimp shells to create a flavorful stock that you can use as a base for fish soup or as a substitute in recipes that call for clam juice.

Cook the olive oil in a medium saucepan set on medium heat until sizzling, about 2 minutes. Add the shrimp shells, garlic, onion, celery and carrot and cook for 5 minutes. Add the tomato paste, parsley and thyme, increase the heat to high and cook for 2 more minutes, stirring well. Add the wine and cook until it evaporates, about 3 minutes. Add the clam juice, bring to a boil, and simmer for 30 minutes. Taste for salt and pepper.

Strain the stock through a fine mesh strainer. Let come to room temperature, then refrigerate. It will keep for 4 days in the refrigerator or 1 month in the freezer.

PANE GRATTUGIATO CONDITO

ITALIAN BREAD CRUMBS

Homemade bread crumbs are just as tasty as the ones you buy at the store and a lot less salty. They're also a creative recycling use for stale bread.

Makes 1½ cups

INGREDIENTS
½ teaspoon olive oil
1 cup plain bread crumbs
1 tablespoon finely chopped fresh basil
1 tablespoon finely chopped fresh parsley
⅛ teaspoon salt
⅛ teaspoon pepper
2 tablespoons grated Romano or Parmigiano Reggiano cheese

Brush a nonstick sauté pan with the olive oil and warm over medium heat for 1 minute. Add the bread crumbs and cook, stirring, until brown, about 2 minutes.

Transfer to a bowl, add all the remaining ingredients and mix well. Let the mixture come to room temperature, then store in an airtight container or reclosable plastic bag.

INDICE

Index

CIAÓ A TUTTI! (HI EVERYBODY!)
THANK YOU FOR CHOOSING
MY CUCINA AMORE COOKBOOK.
I BELIEVE THAT I CAN
LEARN NEW AND EXCITING IDEAS
FROM YOUR EXPERIMENTS WITH
MY RECIPES. LET'S START OUR
RELATIONSHIP BY FILLING OUT
THE COUPON BELOW. I PROMISE
TO KEEP YOU INFORMED OF NEW
CUCINA AMORE DEVELOPMENTS
AND PRODUCTS.
GRAZIE E ARRIVEDERCI,

NICK STELLINO
CUCINA AMORE

NON TI SCORDAR DIME! (DON'T FORGET ME!)
I WANT TO DISCOVER MORE NEW IDEAS FROM CUCINA AMORE!

MY NAME

ADDRESS

CITY   STATE/ZIP

PHONE NUMBER (OPTIONAL): (   )
               AREA CODE

CUCINA AMORE

Detach and mail to: Cucina Amore, Dept. 201, Post Office Box 84848, Seattle, WA 98124